TREVOR WYE
&
PATRICIA MORRIS

The
Orchestral
Flute
Practice
Book 1

*With thanks to the Librarians of the BBC Symphony Orchestra
for their unfailing support, patience and kindness*

Exclusive distributors:

Hal Leonard
7777 West Bluemound Road, Milwaukee, WI 53213
Email: info@halleonard.com
Hal Leonard Europe Limited
42 Wigmore Street Maryleborne, London, WIU 2 RN
Email: info@halleonardeurope.com
Hal Leonard Australia Pty. Ltd.
4 Lentara Court Cheltenham, Victoria, 9132 Australia
Email: info@halleonard.com.au

All rights reserved.
Order No. NOV120801
ISBN 0-85360-806-7
© Copyright 1998 Novello & Company Limited.

Music processed by Barnes Music Engraving.
Book design by Pearce Marchbank, Studio Twenty.

Printed in EU.

www.halleonard.com

CONTENTS

PREFACE

It has always struck us as odd that in conservatories and colleges of music throughout the world, we learn the repertoire for flute and piano much more thoroughly than the orchestral repertoire. Yet professionally, very, very few flute players are able to support themselves as soloists. Of course, the repertoire for flute and piano is more self-contained and therefore more satisfying to practise. So, in order to encourage the would-be orchestral player to work at these extracts regularly, we have presented the important solos with 'cue lines' to help them understand the 'background'. We hope our efforts will help important solos come alive.

Try as we might, we couldn't begin to compile the complete orchestral vade mecum because, even as you are reading this, more is being written! All the same, these two volumes contain a large proportion of the major orchestral material that a player will encounter, as well as some they are unlikely to play! Times and fashions change for composers, too: orchestral managers, conductors and impresarios all have their current favourite repertoire and what may be an important orchestral work today could be forgotten tomorrow. So with that in mind, we have included all the major orchestral repertoire and in addition we have included some which were once popular and could reappear.

Many passages which are not 'solo' in the real sense of the word are also included, because we are sure you will be grateful for a look at the notes before the first rehearsal. Some lesser known solos are included to enable you to consider musical style and the use of different tone colours which are available in the flute's palette.

Cue lines have been included as a guide and a reminder as to what else is happening in the orchestra during the big moment. However helpful this cue line may prove, it can't replace a look at the score. If you haven't played it or heard it before try to listen to a recording, though it doesn't take the place of real orchestral experience. If at all possible, listen with the score so that you'll have some sense of the whole piece into which the solo fits. The cue lines have been transposed into 'C' in the treble clef, to facilitate easier reference. (In doing this, relative octaves have been ignored.)

This book is divided into 7 sections, each of which features specific orchestral or sectional problems. The last is a general section, which covers the remaining standard repertoire you need to cover. Volume 1 covers composers A to M; Volume 2 features N to Z. Where possible, we have tried to keep all the excerpts from one work together in the same section, to make practising easier. However, where works contain specific examples of orchestral difficulties, we have grouped these together so that a particular aspect of orchestral playing can be focused on and studied.

WHERE TO START

There is a lot of music in these two volumes, and to be realistic - because of individual preferences of both conductors and orchestral managements - some of it you may never play. We suggest you start with the most popular ones in the list THE TOP TWENTY-EIGHT. If you have any major technical difficulties such as articulation, playing softly in the third octave, or fingering problems, then we recommend that you work firstly with appropriate material such as articulation exercises or tone studies*. The reason for this is that if you practise an orchestral passage purely as an exercise, you are likely to play it like that in an orchestra, losing its interest and vitality. So remove any major problems with suitable exercises, and then these extracts shouldn't be too problematic.

Practise memorising the big tunes in different keys where that is possible. On returning to the original key, one often finds more flexibility and freedom of expression than before (advice which Marcel Moyse advocated when learning a difficult or important solo). Try to include an orchestral excerpt each day as a part of your practise routine, rather than having a periodic burst at half a dozen. In addition, it's valuable to work at a contemporary extract as part of your daily schedule. Some of the more common and harmonically simple extracts should be memorised, such as the Mendelssohn 'Scherzo' and 'L'après midi d'un faune'. That will allow you to try them out at any time and place, perhaps as warm-ups, without getting the book out to practise.

* Trevor Wye's Practice Books For The Flute Volumes 1 to 6 (Novellos)

TOP OF THE POPS

Recent surveys of orchestral audition lists have revealed the popularity of some pieces which we have called 'Top of The Pops'. Of course, fashions change in orchestral concert planning and a number of people are involved in selecting audition pieces: the leader, the conductor, the orchestral management and the flute section. A good indication of what might be given as sight-reading is a look at the recent programmes of the orchestra for which you are auditioning.

This list is approximately in order of international audition popularity at the time of writing, and there is no reason to expect it to change very much in the forseeable future. It goes without saying that the top twenty-eight should be thoroughly learned - not just for the upcoming audition, but as a future investment:. To have these pieces tucked in your belt is to be well prepared.

THE TOP TWENTY-EIGHT
According to popularity:

1	Ravel	DAPHNIS ET CHLOÉ
2	Debussy	PRÉLUDE À L'APRÈS MIDI D'UN FAUNE
3	Beethoven	OVERTURE: LEONORE No.3
4	Mendelssohn	SCHERZO from A MIDSUMMER NIGHT'S DREAM
5	Brahms	SYMPHONY No.4
6	Prokofiev	CLASSICAL SYMPHONY
7	R Strauss	TILL EULENSPIEGELS
8	Prokofiev	PETER AND THE WOLF
9	Saint-Saëns	VOLIERE from CARNIVAL OF THE ANIMALS
10	Tchaikovsky	SYMPHONY No.4
11	Dvorák	SYMPHONY IN G MAJOR
12	Bartók	CONCERTO FOR ORCHESTRA
13	Rimsky-Korsakov	SHEHERAZADE
14	Stravinsky	PETROUCHKA
15	Berlioz	SYMPHONIE FANTASTIQUE
16	Brahms	SYMPHONY No.1
17	Beethoven	SYMPHONY No.3
18	Stravinsky	FIREBIRD SUITE
19	Stravinsky	SONG OF THE NIGHTINGALE
20	Hindemith	SYMPHONIC METAMORPHOSES
21	Britten	SEA INTERLUDES
22	R Strauss	SALOME
23	Bizet	ENTR'ACTE from CARMEN
24	Prokofiev	LIEUTENANT KIJÉ
25	Prokofiev	ROMEO AND JULIET
26	Ravel	BOLERO*
27	Rossini	'WILLIAM TELL' OVERTURE
28	JS Bach	No.58 FROM THE ST MATTHEW PASSION

* No extracts from this work are included in these volumes.

ALSO LIKELY TO APPEAR
In alphabetical order:

JS Bach	ST. JOHN PASSION
Beethoven	SYMPHONIES Nos.1, 6 & 7
Borodin	POLOTSVIAN DANCES
Brahms	SYMPHONY No.3
Britten	THE YOUNG PERSON'S GUIDE TO THE ORCHESTRA
Debussy	LA MER
	NOCTURNES
Dvořák	'NEW WORLD' SYMPHONY
Gluck	DANCE OF THE BLESSED SPIRITS
	from ORFEO ED EURIDICE
Kodály	PEACOCK VARIATIONS
Mahler	DAS LIED VON DER ERDE (last movement)
Mendelssohn	SYMPHONY No.4
Musorgsky	NIGHT ON THE BARE MOUNTAIN
Piston	THE INCREDIBLE FLUTIST
Prokofiev	SYMPHONY No.5
Ravel	MOTHER GOOSE SUITE
	LA VALSE
Reznicek	DONNA DIANA OVERTURE
Rimsky-Korsakov	CAPRICCIO ESPAGNOLE
	RUSSIAN EASTER OVERTURE
Rossini	THE BARBER OF SEVILLE
	OVERTURES (various)
	SEMIRAMIDE
Schubert	SYMPHONIES Nos.5 & 9
Schumann	SYMPHONY No.1
Shostakovich	SYMPHONIES Nos.1, 5, 6, 10, & 15
Smetana	THE BARTERED BRIDE OVERTURE
R Strauss	EIN HELDENLEBEN
	SYMPHONIA DOMESTICA
Stravinsky	DUMBARTON OAKS
	THE FAIRY'S KISS
	THE RITE OF SPRING
	SONG OF THE NIGHTINGALE
	SYMPHONY IN 3 MOVEMENTS
Tchaikovsky	THE NUTCRACKER SUITE
	PIANO CONCERTO No.1 (second movement)
	SYMPHONY No.6
Thomas	MIGNON OVERTURE
Wagner	MAGIC FIRE MUSIC

THE AUDITION

The orchestral management advertises and you reply: by doing so, you are implying that you are just the person they are looking for! A time and place for your audition is agreed upon and from that moment, it's your responsibility to prove it.

Prepare yourself properly. If you are relatively (or even completely) inexperienced, it's not enough to simply learn the notes. You need to know how your part fits into the accompanying orchestral texture, and you must reflect this knowledge in your performance of the passage. Always take a piccolo; the principal player is sometimes required to change to the piccolo, and a reasonable ability on it is usually a requirement. If you have arrived early, don't be put off by what you can hear of the person already in mid-audition. Everyone sounds good through closed doors!

Rhythm is the most important point to remember about any sight-reading you may be given. This is especially critical in long notes and trills - it's so easy to lose track of the beat. Keep all long notes for their full value, even if exceptionally long. If you are given what is in fact 'real' sight-reading (something you have never seen before) concentrate on the correct rhythm as well as the right notes. Look upon rhythm as a priority. In an orchestra, if you were to play a rhythm incorrectly (and that includes miscounting rests or long notes) or enter in the wrong place, you may well upset someone else's entry who has been following your cue in their part.

Your solo with piano: unless you take your own pianist to the audition, you will have to rely on the staff pianist engaged by the orchestral management. These accompanists are usually (but not always) competent; normally there is no rehearsal so you will only have a few seconds to discuss tempi, etc. The accompanist may or may not be familiar with your solo, so to be on the safe side, don't choose a piece with a really difficult piano part or one which they are unlikely to know . You will probably feel more secure in your musical performance if you take your own pianist with whom you have rehearsed.

Sometimes the panel specify the solo, sometimes not. If you have a free choice, the most usual solos are the Mozart Concerti (one of which is normally specified), the Ibert and Nielsen Concerti and the Prokofiev Sonata. Other frequently played pieces are the works of Hüe, Fauré, Enesco, Dutilleux, Messiaen, Poulenc, Bozza, Gaubert, Ibert ('Pièce'), Martin and Widor. If you are asked to choose two contrasting pieces, you should choose one classical piece to show your sense of style plus a modern or Romantic piece to show off your variety of tone colours and virtuosity. Your choice must demonstrate what you are capable of!

If you are auditioning for a second flute position, how would you approach your solo? Do you play the Prokofiev Flute Sonata like a second flautist? No, but you can reflect in your performance the attributes of a good second flute player. For example, a good, firm, in-tune low register would help, as would the ability to play very softly and in tune with a varied vibrato. Musical sensitivity, a sense of the style of different periods, and attention paid to dynamics, accents, lengths of notes and articulation would all be suggestive of flexibility in a positive way. A big-toned aggressive performance probably wouldn't be advantageous; the principal player wants a colleague who will support them and fit in with the section, not someone who is overly ambitious and wishing they were in the principal's job! An inflexible and heavy vibrato would also be a disadvantage.

'The orchestra obviously wants someone who is experienced... But how do I become experienced if I can't get a job in the first place?' This is a question frequently asked by students. You can accomplish a great deal by concert going, by taking on the meanest work just for the experience, and by listening frequently to the radio and to recordings. Don't pass up the opportunity to play any kind of chamber music, or indeed flute duets, trios or quartets. These can be a fruitful ground for ensemble and intonation practice. Marcel Moyse once said that flute duets were his only orchestral experience until he joined an orchestra.

IMPOSSIBLE TRILLS

There are a few instances of 'impossible' trills in the repertoire, such as between low C and C♯, but even these can be judiciously 'arranged' so that they become possible! The trill between low C to C♯, for example, can be played by using the inside of your right knee to hold down the C♯ key. It's then simple to trill with just the C lever! The same trick can be accomplished with the trill from C♯ to D♯. With two or more players in the section, the parts can be swopped around so that the player on the right of the 'impossible trill' can play one-handed whilst holding down a key on the flute to their left (provided this is out of sight of the audience!). Alternatively, the use of an elastic band to temporarily hold down a key can get you out of trouble. There is usually some way around an impossible trill. (A full list of trills with alternatives can be found elsewhere.*)

DIFFICULT PASSAGES

A few composers have written passages without being informed about the problems of actually playing them! A good orchestral player will be aware of possible alternative fingering; using harmonics, for example. It would be wise to familiarise yourself with these if you haven't already done so. Start on low C and, using the second harmonic (or overtone), play a chromatic scale. Apart from the first four notes, the rest are all the same as the usual fingering in the second octave. Now repeat this scale using the third harmonic as the starting note. Follow this by using the fourth and fifth harmonics as starting notes. As you go higher up, the number of notes becomes more restricted, but these notes can sometimes get you out of trouble.

You aren't using the correct fingering? There is no such thing. The correct fingering is the one that gives the best and smoothest result. The orchestral position will go to the most competent player - not necessarily to the one who fingers the flute according to the fingering chart.

* Trevor Wye's Practice Book For The Flute Volume 6 (NOV120591)

Section One

LONG SOLOS AND BREATH CONTROL

These extracts won't in themselves help much with any problems you have with control and longevity of breathing: they are here to show some of the problems an orchestral player is faced with. Advice for these problems can be found elsewhere. In solos such as the two Debussy extracts, you can check your progress in these areas on a weekly basis. Posture, fitness, and really *wanting* to succeed all play a part.

See also:

Bach	St John Passion No. 63	General Section, Book 1
Bach	Mass in B minor, Gloria – Domine Deus	Section 2, Book 1
Bartók	Concerto for Orchestra	Section 2, Book 1
Mendelssohn	A Midsummer Night's Dream, Scherzo	Section 2, Book 1
Musorgsky	Night on a Bare Mountain	Section 1, Book 2
Ravel	Shéhérazade, La Flûte Enchantée	General Section, Book 2
Schumann	Piano Concerto in A minor	Section 1, Book 2
Stravinsky	The Fairy's Kiss, Prologue	General Section, Book 2

THE BANKS OF GREEN WILLOW

A *dolce* 'folk song' tone is required without excessive emotion, so play with a gentle vibrato.

PRÉLUDE À 'L'APRÈS-MIDI D'UN FAUNE'

In some orchestras, it has become common to expect the performer to play the opening solo in one breath. Yet some conductors insist on one or two breaths and even specify where these will be. In our opinion, the number of breaths is unimportant so long as the overall 'line' is maintained. This music wasn't written to be performed as a circus trick.

On stage, prepare for the solo by overblowing low C♯ into its second harmonic. This will give you the pitch of the first C♯.

A common mistake is to forget the duplet on the second note, which is in effect a syncopation, and a common device in the works of Debussy and Ravel.

The conductor will not usually beat the opening solo, but will indicate to you to begin when you are ready.

See also the rest of the extract in Section Two (p.35).

PETITE SUITE

En bateau

Try to avoid 'bumping' in orchestral playing – creating unwanted accents which spoils the flow or 'line' of the phrase. A typical place where 'bumping' should be avoided is on the second beat of the second bar. Breathing suggestions are added and the (✓) is an alternative.

The articulation in bar 23, *portato*, should be carefully observed.

DEBUSSY

SYMPHONY NO. 8

4th Movement

There is a loud tutti immediately preceding this solo and this should always be included as part of your practice strategy. In an orchestral performance though, the last two bars of the orchestral tutti are usually omitted by the principal player whilst the second player simply plays louder!

There are many ways of tackling where to breathe. Here are three suggestions:
a – For those who can play long phrases without too much trouble.
b – For the average player.
c – For those who have no great lung capacity.
(x indicates a poor place to breathe musically.)

It is also important in your practice to make the piece louder and slower than you might expect. This allows for the peculiarities of the conductor's tempi, and also the fact that it takes far more resonance to project over the orchestra than it does to be effective at home! You will also then find it easier to play well if the conductor does set a comfortable tempo and balances the orchestra well.

DVOŘÁK

L'ALLEGRO, IL PENSEROSO ED IL MODERATO

'Sweet Bird' No. 12, Part 1

We have reproduced only part of this long solo. Though much of it involves only basic scales and arpeggios so seems easy, it should be practised without stopping in order to test your stamina and breathing. The articulation is part of the interpretation: you may choose to slur some of the semiquavers.

HANDEL

SYMPHONY NO. 102 IN B♭ MAJOR

2nd Movement

Check that the ornaments are played correctly.

HAYDN

SYMPHONY NO. 9

4th Movement

Ab *pianissimo* and top A can be sharpened by adding the low C♯ key.

MAHLER

FANTASIA ON 'GREENSLEEVES'

(adapted from *Sir John in Love*)

The breathing is not so difficult to manage if you play *pianissimo*. Often the second flute takes over the middle F in the cadenza* to facilitate this long solo.

VAUGHAN WILLIAMS

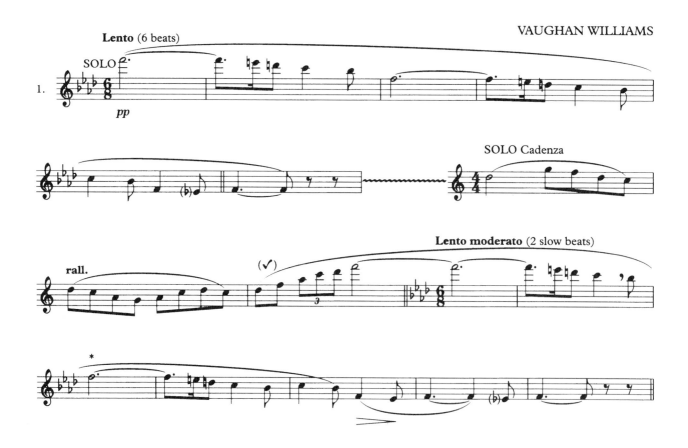

Section Two

THE BIG TUNES

The 'cue lines' given in this section are for you to take in and observe the other parts as you are playing the big tune. It's better to learn these tunes from memory – then you can obtain more freedom of expression and sensitivity by a greater awareness of the accompaniment. In some of the solos, it might help to record the accompaniment on the piano – it's not important if the notes are at the wrong octave – but at least it will provide a rhythmic and harmonic background to the solo. If you take up this suggestion, use a metronome to keep the tempo steady.

See also:

Beethoven	Symphony No. 4	General Section, Book 1
Beethoven	Symphony No. 6	Section 1, Book 2
Britten	Sinfonietta, Variations & Tarantella	General Section, Book 1
Debussy	La Mer	General Section, Book 1
Musorgsky	Night on a Bare Mountain	Section 1, Book 2
Prokofiev	Lieutenant Kijé	General Section, Book 1
Ravel	Shéhérazade	General Section, Book 2
Strauss (R.)	Ein Heldenleben	Section 4, Book 2
Stravinsky	The Fairy's Kiss,	General Section, Book 2
Tchaikovsky	The Nutcracker Suite,	General Section, Book 2
Tchaikovsky	Piano Concerto No. 1	General Section, Book 2
Vaughan Williams	Symphony No. 6	General Section, Book 2

We recommend you get a full score if possible, otherwise a vocal score would be helpful. Read the words of the aria or obbligato solo you are to play: it will help you to understand what is happening at that moment and will provide some clues as to your interpretation.

ST MATTHEW PASSION

No. 58. Aria: Aus Liebe will mein Heiland sterben

A common feature of 18th century music was the use of the flute to depict grief and sadness. In this instance, Bach gives the flute an important obbligato solo just before the Crucifixion. The two throbbing oboi da caccia perhaps represent the heartbeat of Christ over which the flute plays this poignant and beautiful solo.

Be sure to play the correct rhythm in the first bar and be prepared to change the appoggiaturas according to a conductor's wishes. (Then having spent some time preparing for your big moment, you may learn at the first rehearsal that No. 49 is to be cut!)

JS BACH

16

MASS IN B MINOR

Bach can contain the most unexpected harmonies. . . when faced with an entire page in $\frac{3}{2}$ time in which the two flutes were playing a duo very slowly on the second and third beats of the bar, one player looked up at the conductor for a few moments and then back again at the page. . . but he was lost. After several attempts to find the right place, each of which sounded wrong, he whispered to his colleague, 'Where are we?' In the next beat rest, his friend whispered, 'The Festival Hall'.

GLORIA

Domine Deus

Just the kind of solo everyone plays well at home in the kitchen, but are left breathless both at the rehearsal and performance. In this kind of solo, you must pace yourself: avoid long passages without a breath – unless you can do this comfortably. We have indicated sensible breathing places. Take more frequent breaths to begin with. Always play the entire solo through before the first rehearsal to test your breathing and stamina.

JS BACH

18

20

Qui tollis

22

BENEDICTUS

This is sometimes played as a violin solo. Opinions vary about appoggiaturas according to the orchestral style: it would be wise to look into this before the rehearsal.

CONCERTO FOR ORCHESTRA

I Introduzione

Note the accents, dynamics, dots and rhythms.

BARTÓK

II Giuoco delle coppie

III Elegia

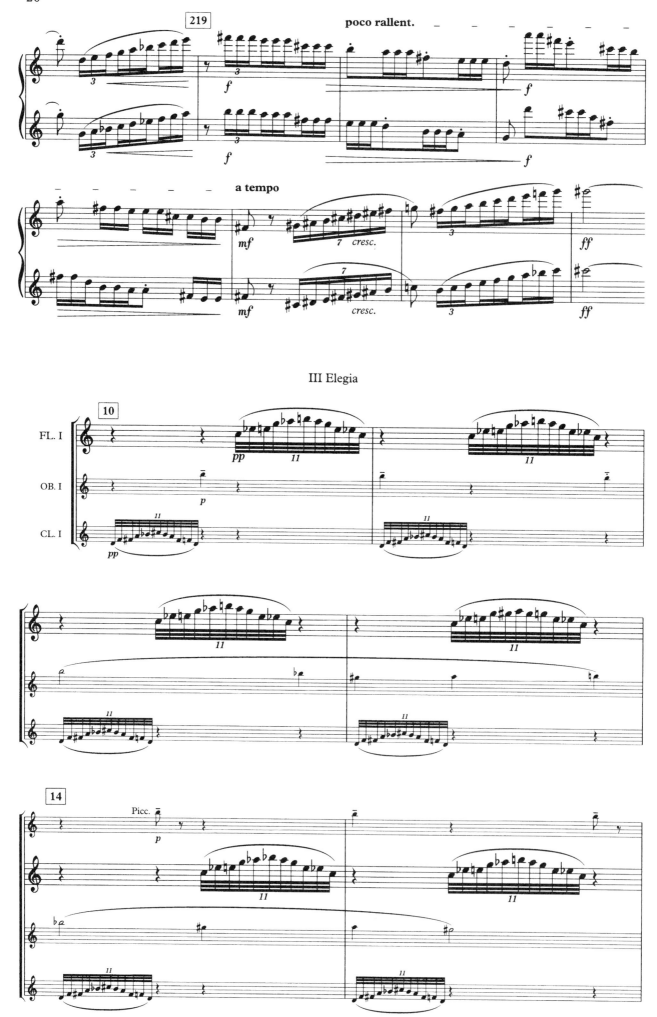

IV Intermezzo interrotto

V Finale

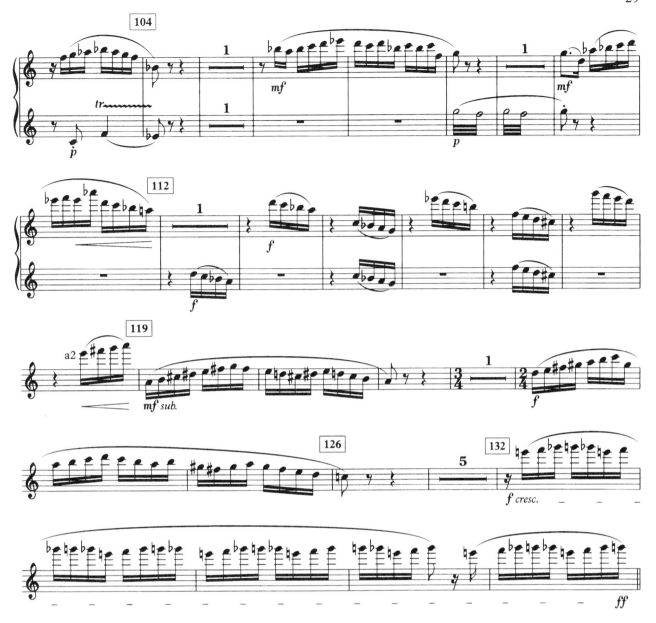

OVERTURE 'LEONORE NO. 3'

Allow enough time in the fast section for the bassoon scale. In an audition, always complete the long 'D' at the end.

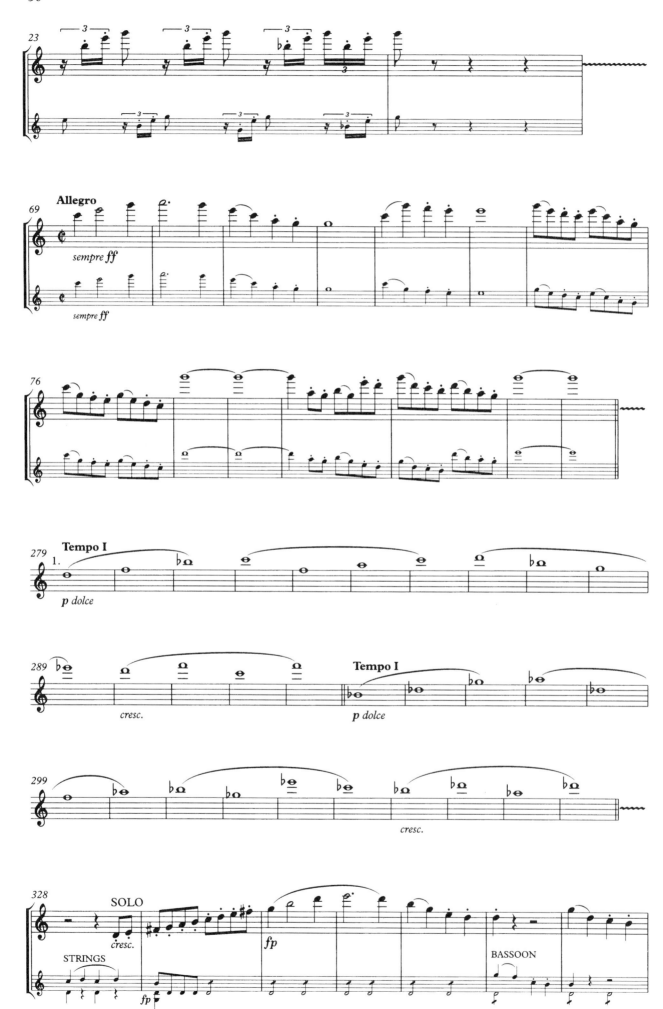

32

L'ARLÉSIENNE

Suite No. 2

III Menuet

Avoid messing about with the rhythm too much in this solo: keep it simple and cheerful. The opening is marked *pianissimo* – start it off that way. In this solo and in the *Entra'cte* from Carmen, top E♭ will usually sound sharp: flatten it. Keep the tempo steady throughout the solo.

BIZET

SYMPHONY NO. 1

4th Movement

Practise making a really big sound here – one which matches the French horns. Top E is usually sharp and in this key it sounds better if it is flat. (It will help to play it flatter if you don't use your D♯ key.) You would be wise to pull the headjoint out before this solo.

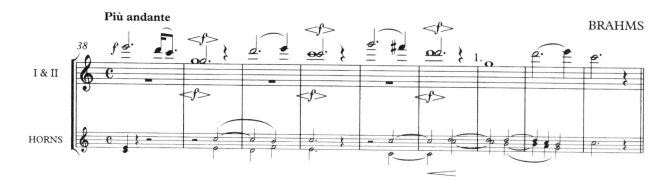

SYMPHONY NO. 4

2nd Movement

Don't use excessive vibrato during the opening descending scale. In fact, in an audition, be prepared to be asked not to use vibrato! Observe the use of appoggiaturas in this solo. Try playing with a metronome to avoid pulling it around too much.

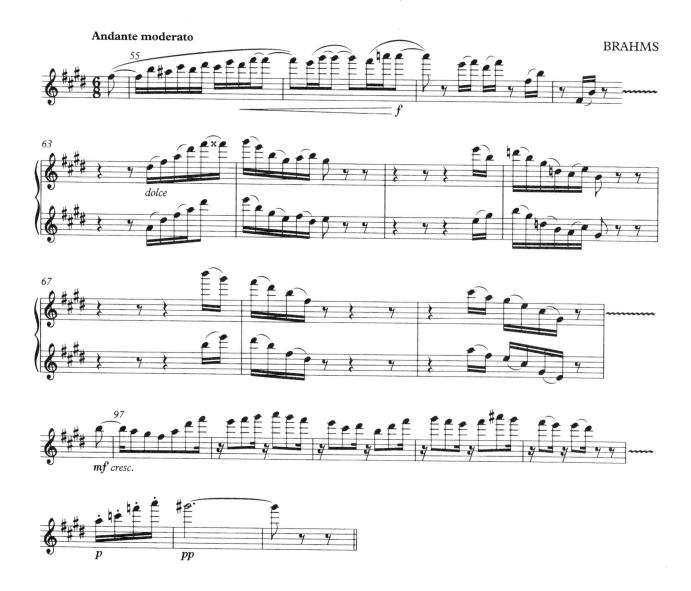

4th Movement

PRÉLUDE À 'L'APRÈS-MIDI D'UN FAUNE'

Be prepared to be flexible. A full score is essential to understand what the rest of the section is doing. In popular pieces like this, conductors may try something different in order to make their mark.

DEBUSSY

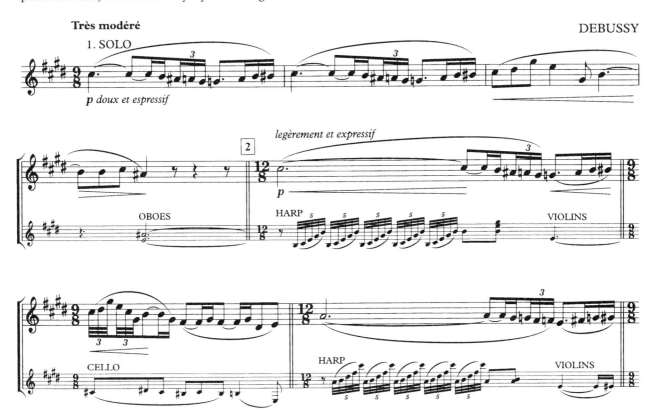

36

38

SYMPHONY NO. 8

Op. 88

1st Movement

You need a clear, singing tone and a good staccato with nimble trills in the section which follows.

DVOŘÁK

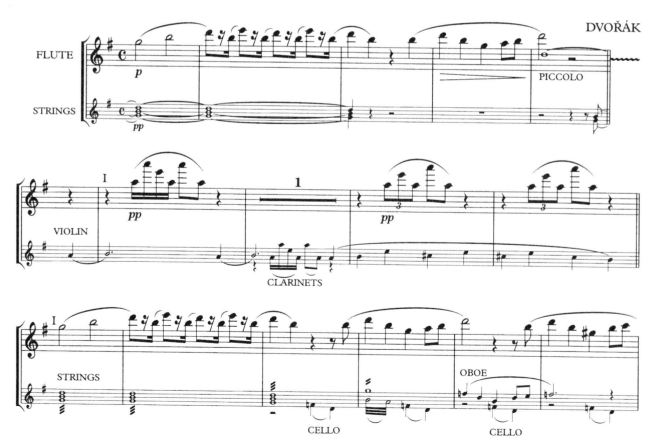

2nd Movement

40

3rd Movement

4th Movement

etc.

SYMPHONY NO. 9

From the New World, Op. 95

1st Movement

Some testing low solos in the 1st Movement.

DVOŘÁK

2nd Movement

3rd Movement (Scherzo)

DANCE OF THE BLESSED SPIRITS

from 'Orfeo'

Be sure you fully understand what appoggiaturas are and how to play them. In bar 15, the slur with dots is an indication that the line is to be maintained: resist the impulse to take audible breaths here. In the eighth bar the rhythm may be somewhat different than you are used to seeing. The original version of the scale is printed below. Be prepared for either version.

GLUCK

* This is the original

SYMPHONIC METAMORPHOSES

II Turandot, Scherzo

Practise to acquire smooth and even tone in the legato triplets. The trills should all be at the same speed.

HINDEMITH

III Andantino

Practise this with the cue line to familiarise yourself with the accompanying parts; in that way, it is easier to understand the ebb and flow of the tempo.

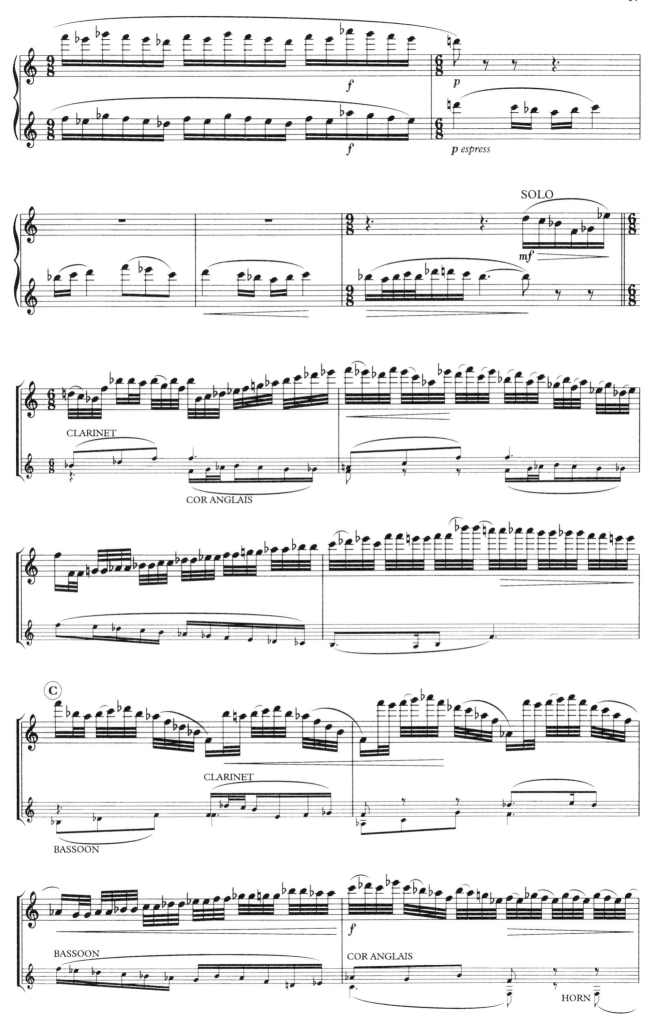

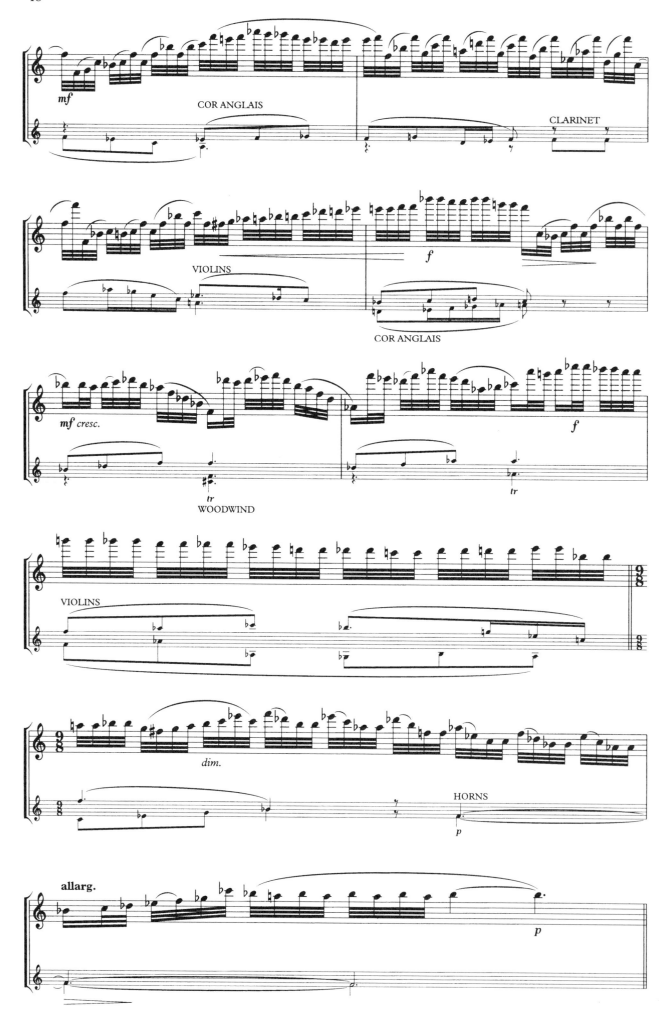

DAS LIED VON DER ERDE

2. Der Einsame im Herbst

We recommend you listen to a good recording as well, to really get to know this work.

MAHLER

sempre *pp*

nie - der

pp

mit sei-nen Schat - ten, die voll Küh - lung

sind.

morendo *p* *sf* *p*

CONTRABASSOON

sf *p*

I

II

sf

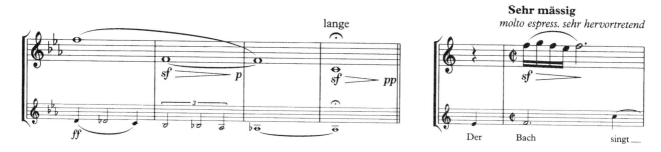

sf *p*

ff

lange

sf *p*

sf *pp*

Sehr mässig
molto espress. sehr hervortretend

sf

Der Bach singt

sf *p* *tr*

3 3 3 3 3

vol - ler Wohl - laut durch das Dun - kel.

3

Etwas bewegter
1.2.3.
zu 3

3

f

cresc.

3 3

VIOLINS

p

Die Blu - men blas - sen im Däm - mer - schein.

SCHERZO

from 'A Midsummer Night's Dream'

It is wise to practise this by varying the speed from your fastest single tonguing up to double tonguing. Different tempi provide different problems, especially in breathing. Although you can play for longer at a faster tempo, the space in which to snatch a breath is shorter.

A common mistake is to play this too quickly at auditions, so practise with a metronome to keep the solo steady. In bar 365, leave out the first G if you can't manage the rest of the solo in one breath – this note is covered by the woodwind at that point. You must not breathe between here and the end of the solo. Don't attempt to play from bars 359 through to 377 without a breath unless completely confident.

MENDELSSOHN

52

PETER AND THE WOLF

Op. 67

Check that you can play this solo fast and fluently. Don't neglect the other fragments such as the passage five bars after figure 30.

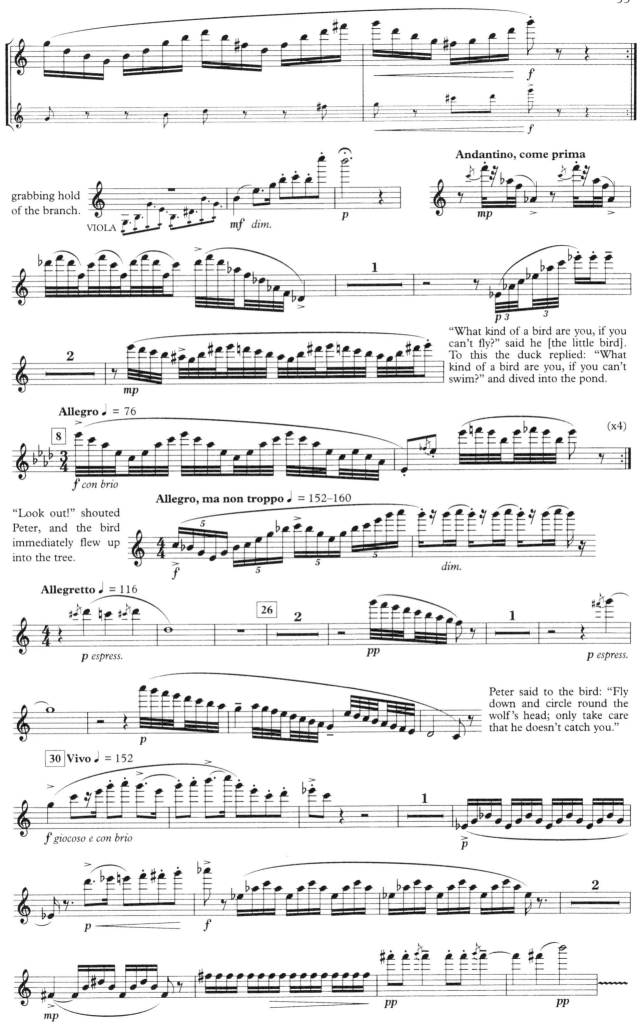

grabbing hold of the branch.

VIOLA

Andantino, come prima

"What kind of a bird are you, if you can't fly?" said he [the little bird]. To this the duck replied: "What kind of a bird are you, if you can't swim?" and dived into the pond.

Allegro ♩ = 76

"Look out!" shouted Peter, and the bird immediately flew up into the tree.

Allegro, ma non troppo ♩ = 152–160

Allegretto ♩ = 116

Peter said to the bird: "Fly down and circle round the wolf's head; only take care that he doesn't catch you."

30 Vivo ♩ = 152

54

Following the wolf's trail and shooting as they went.

Above them flew birdie chirping merrily: "My, what brave fellows we are, Peter and I! Look what we have caught!"

DAPHNIS ET CHLOÉ

It is better to learn this without any preconceived ideas about phrasing. First, work at it with a metronome to be sure that the rhythms are clearly understood before indulging in 'rubato'. Learn that first scale thoroughly so you can play it confidently without a blemish. Regarding the first E♯: according to Marcel Moyse, who played in the première, he asked the conductor, "Is that an E♯ or E♮?" The conductor in turn asked Ravel, who merely shrugged, indicating that he was indifferent. Contrary to popular legend, he didn't speak.

RAVEL

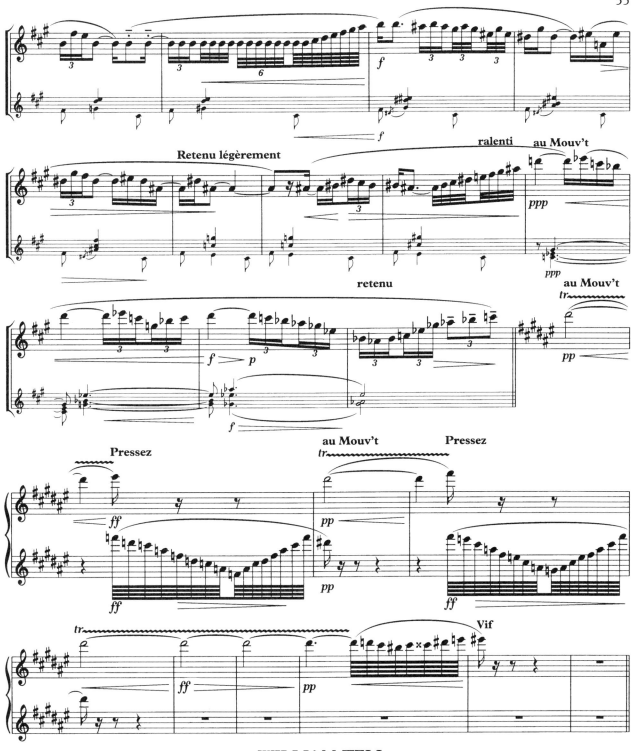

WILLIAM TELL
Overture

Avoid tied-note accents ('bumping') and take care to play the full three beats on all trills. In bar 209 on, *aim* to play on the beat – this seems to help.

ROSSINI

SEMIRAMIDE

Overture

The grace notes need to be played quickly.

ROSSINI

58

THE CARNIVAL OF THE ANIMALS

No.10 Volière

Excellent articulation is paramount in this famous solo. If you are 'in extremis', or are having difficulty maintaining a consistent rhythmic staccato, a judicious slurring of two notes here and there may help to maintain the flow. When practising, a slur may help to bring the low notes out in the bars before figures 3 and 4.

SAINT-SAËNS

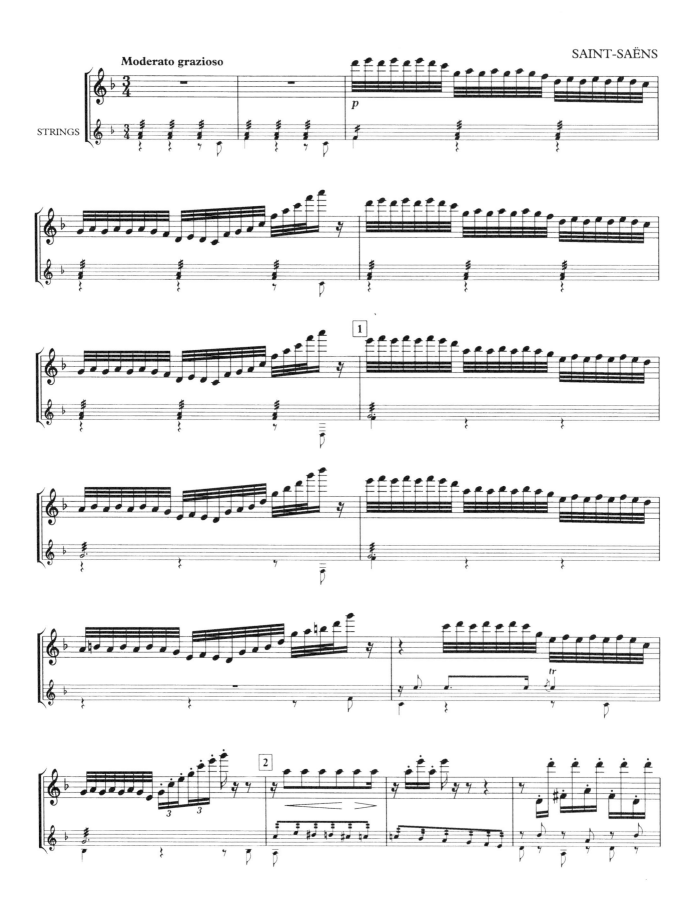

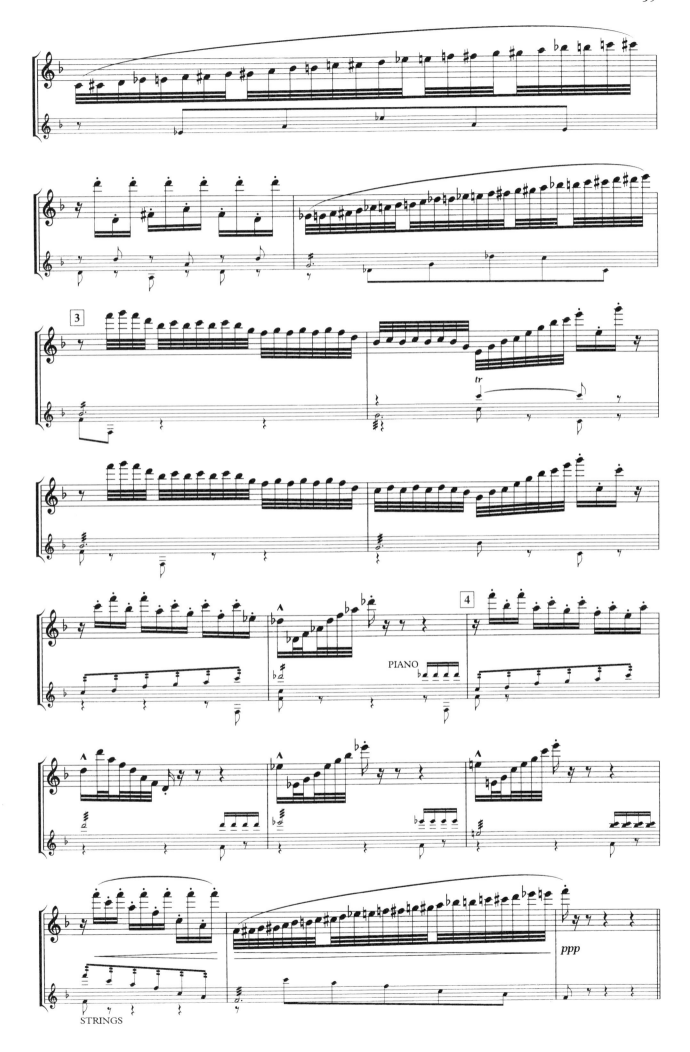

STRINGS

SALOME

Scene IV

This sensuous dance needs special thought, but before learning how to play sensuously, check it with a metronome for rhythmic accuracy!

R. STRAUSS

* See p.XX for a glossary of German terms.

SLEEPING BEAUTY

Act III, No.25: Pas de quatre

'Bluebird Variation'

A beautiful tone quality coupled with a clean technique is needed here. First practise the skeleton of the melody in the groups of six, as in many solos of this kind: G, E, C, G (shown by *). Practise these outline notes for sonority and colour, adding the remaining notes only when the tone colour can be preserved.

TCHAIKOVSKY

62

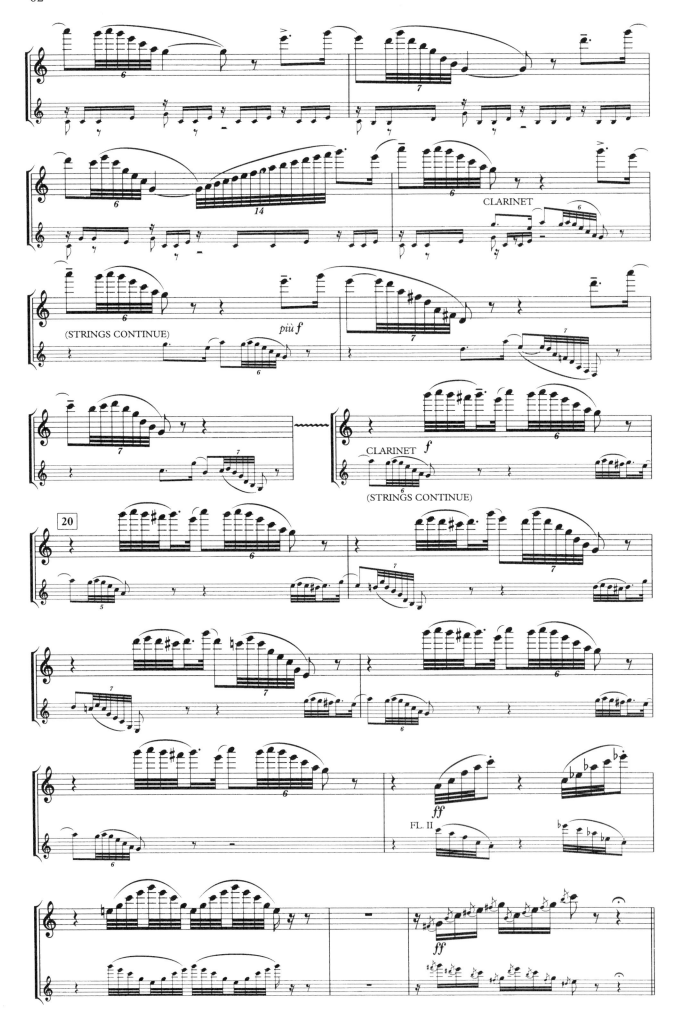

Section Three

ARTICULATION PASSAGES

Most audition panels will include a solo to enable the candidates to demonstrate their articulation skills. Articulation is the language of music. If you have problems in this area, you must get down to some serious practise on articulation, rather than just work at these passages. Save them until your skill improves.

See also:

Beethoven	Symphony No. 9	General Section, Book 1
Delius	Brigg Fair	Section 1, Book 2
Mendelssohn	Symphony No. 4 (4th movt)	Section 3, Book 2
	Overture Calm Sea and Prosperous Voyage	General Section, Book 1
Prokofiev	Classical Symphony (4th movt)	General Section, Book 1
Rimsky-Korsakov	Sheherazade	General Section, Book 2
Rossini	William Tell Overture	Section 2, Book 1
	Semiramide Overture	Section 2, Book 1
J. Strauss	Die Fledermaus	General Section, Book 2
Saint-Saëns	The Carnival of the Animals: Volière	Section 2, Book 1
Tchaikovsky	Symphony No. 4	General Section, Book 2

ST JOHN PASSION

No. 16d. Chorus: Wir dürfen niemand töten

This passage is famous for unexpected accidentals! Practise until you can sail through it without a mistake.

64

NOCTURNE

(for Tenor, 7 obbligato instruments and string orchestra)

What is more gentle than a wind in summer?

Relaxed and flexible double tonguing is necessary here in order to have the freedom to *rubato* at will. Note the *staccatissimo*, typical of Britten: very dry and precise.

ENIGMA VARIATIONS

II

(H.D.S.–P.)

ELGAR

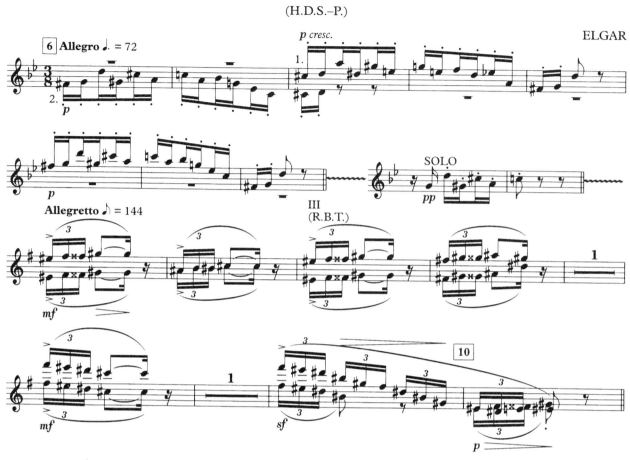

RUSSLAN AND LUDMILLA

Overture

GLINKA

DONNA DIANA

Overture

This is included because of the relentless demands of the articulation.

REZNICEK

68

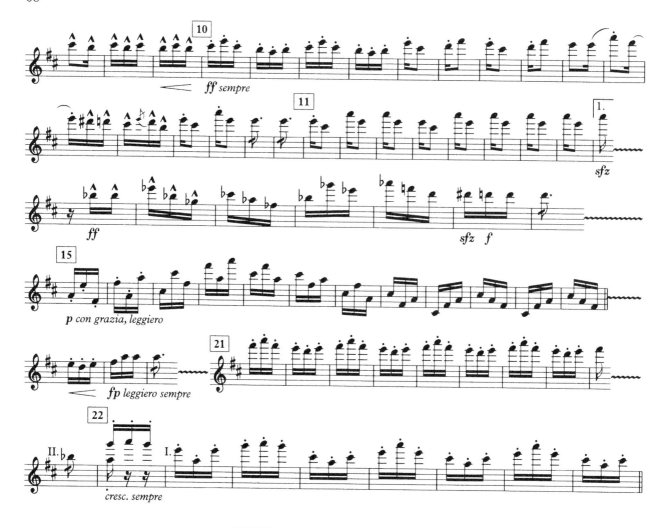

THE THIEVISH MAGPIE

(La gazza ladra)

Overture

ROSSINI

THE BARTERED BRIDE

Overture

Practise the opening with a metronome. It usually goes very quickly.

SMETANA

DUMBARTON OAKS

Concerto in E♭

1st Movement

STRAVINSKY

2nd Movement

CARNIVAL IN PARIS

Overture

This is a short passage, but worth practising to make sure the grace notes cut sharply against the eighth notes (quavers).

VARIATIONS ON A ROCOCO THEME

For Cello and Orchestra

TCHAIKOVSKY

72

Section Four

PIANISSIMO PASSAGES

The idea here is to avoid bad habits! Undue tension, rolling the headjoint in and forgetting about intonation all add to the problems. Always check your intonation, preferably with a tuning machine, when playing very softly.

Other similar passages:

Beethoven	Symphony No. 3 'Eroica'	General Section, Book 1
	Symphony No. 6 'Pastoral'	Section 1, Book 2
	Symphony No. 7	General Section, Book 1
Brahms	Symphony No. 1	General Section, Book 1
	Variations on a Theme of Haydn	General Section, Book 1
Haydn	Symphony No. 102 (slow movt)	Section 1, Book 1
Mendelssohn	A Midsummer Night's Dream Overture	Section 3, Book 2

SYMPHONY NO. 5

2nd Movement

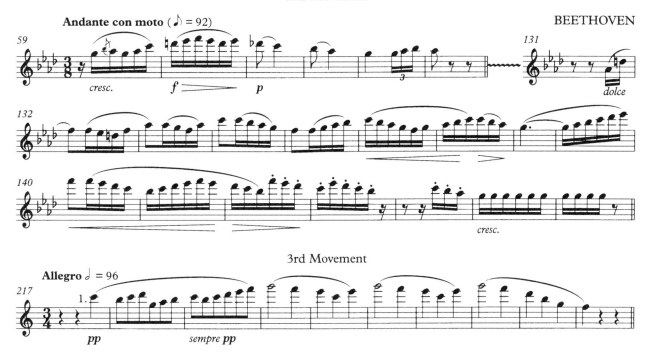

3rd Movement

CARMEN

Act II Entr'acte

Special attention needs to be paid to intonation problems – do try to avoid a sharp top E♭. Try using the special 'Mignon' fingering for top B♭ to obtain a stress-free, soft note.

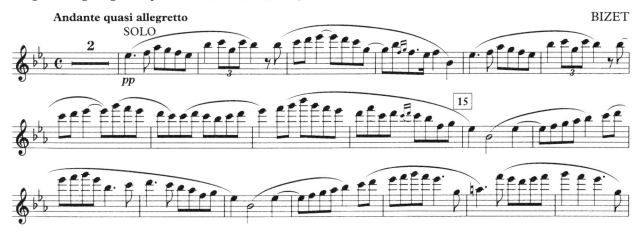

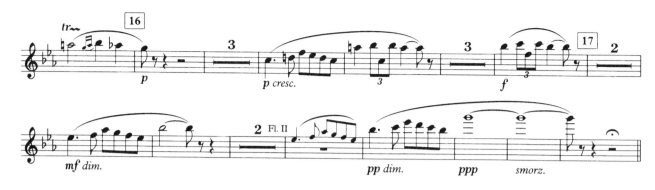

GERMAN REQUIEM

II. Denn alles Fleisch es ist wie Gras

BRAHMS

III. Herr, lehre doch mich

IV. Wie lieblich sind deine Wohnungen

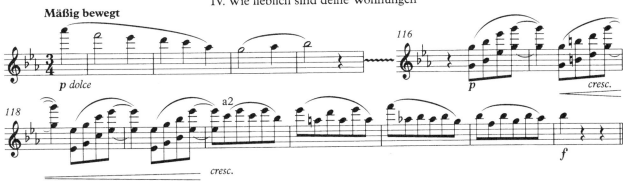

DANCE RHAPSODY NO. 2

DELIUS

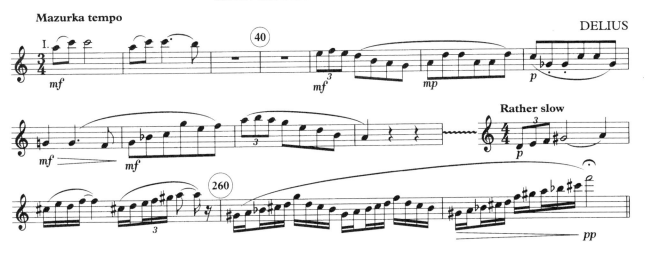

SONG OF SUMMER

DELIUS

THE HEBRIDES, OP. 26

(Fingal's Cave)

Overture

Seemingly easy, yet to play this softly, gently *and* in tune . . .

MENDELSSOHN

REQUIEM

VI. Lux aeterna

The so-called 'Mignon' fingering for top B♭ will be useful. This fingering needs to be practised or you may forget to put the thumb on the B♭ lever (which will result in a B♮!). You need to be sure of your own intonation to allow flexibility with the rest of the orchestra. It is an unfortunate fact that whilst flautists have a tendency to play flat when *pianissimo*, the clarinet has a tendency to be sharp. These are only two examples of the natural proclivities of various instruments!

Section Five

LOW SOLOS

The main problem with low solos is making the flute 'tell' against the other instruments (which may themselves have developed greater amplitude since some of these solos were written). Filling out the low register without sounding 'buzzy' is generally the way forward. Balance the dynamics carefully: the flute naturally sounds softer when it descends and a compensatory *crescendo* may have to be made. Composers use this register for its soft and gentle colour. The trick is to find a colour which will be telling and projects well without forcing the tone.

See also:

Bernstein	West Side Story	General Section, Book 1
Copland	Rodeo	General Section, Book 1
Dvořák	Symphony No. 9	Section 2, Book 1
Mendelssohn	Symphony No. 3 (2nd movt)	General Section, Book 1
Prokofiev	Peter and the Wolf (Figure 39)	Section 2, Book 1
Shostakovich	Symphony No. 10 (1st & 3rd movts)	General Section, Book 2
	Symphony No. 11	General Section, Book 2
Stravinsky	Perséphone	General Section, Book 2
Vaughan Williams	Symphony No. 6	General Section, Book 2

SYMPHONY NO. 7

1st Movement

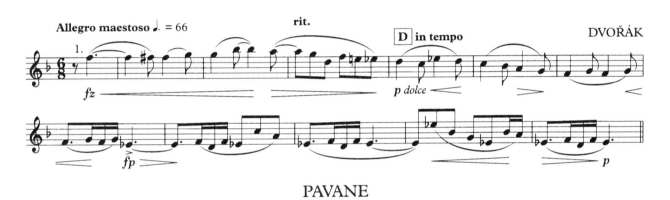

PAVANE

It's not essential to play this in one breath, but better if you can. Use a tone which reflects the sleepy simplicity of the melody.

SHEHERAZADE

Symphonic Suite

IV

RIMSKY-KORSAKOV

EN SAGA

This is a very soft melody, played with clarinet and muted strings.

SIBELIUS

CHANT DU ROSSIGNOL

(The Song of the Nightingale)

STRAVINSKY

SYMPHONIES OF WIND INSTRUMENTS

STRAVINSKY

LA FORZA DEL DESTINO

Overture

VERDI

Section Six

MOZART AND HAYDN

Our instrument has changed a great deal since these works were written. Other orchestral instruments have changed too, the trend being toward bigger, louder and stronger-toned instruments. This should be borne in mind because in the slow movements of Mozart piano concertos there are important solos, often marked *piano* or *pianissimo*. In today's modern orchestras and big concert halls, this can literally mean 'powerful' or 'pretty powerful'!

However, there is a new race of loud players who can easily overdo the dynamics and play too strongly, which in the delicate scoring of Mozart is inappropriate. Fortunately, the views of the historically enlightened players and conductors – the early music specialists – are influencing the 'traditional' orchestras and the scene is constantly changing. *Piano* and *pianissimo* have a wide variety of interpretations depending on a number of factors, including the interpretation the orchestra is used to hearing! Sometimes it's better to ride the horse the way it's going . . . The performer needs to weigh up all the possibilities before making up his or her mind.

These solos are especially sensitive to faulty flute playing. They should be practised with sensitivity and understanding of the full score. Don't underestimate the Haydn *vivace* or *allegro assai*: when the conductor indicates a moderate beat, it will probably be one beat in a bar.

TRUMPET CONCERTO IN E♭ MAJOR

3rd Movement

The flute has to try to match the brilliant and clear articulation of modern trumpet players.

HAYDN

THE CREATION

2. Air with Chorus: Now vanish before the holy beams

HAYDN

15. Air: On mighty pens uplifted soars

27. Trio: On thee each living soul awaits

82

29. Recitative: In rosy mantle appears

30. Hymn: By thee with bliss

DIE JAHRESZEITEN (The Seasons)

Der Frühling (Spring)

4b. Bittgesang: Trio and Chorus: Sei uns gnädig, milder Himmel!

(Be now gracious, o kind heaven!)

HAYDN

Der Sommer (Summer)

9. Recitative: Willkommen jetzt, O dunkler Hain

(O welcome now, ye shady groves)

84

Der Herbst (Autumn)

16b. Chorus: Hört das laute Getön

(Hear the clank and the noise)

17b. Chorus: Juhe, der Wein ist da

(Heyday, the liquor flows)

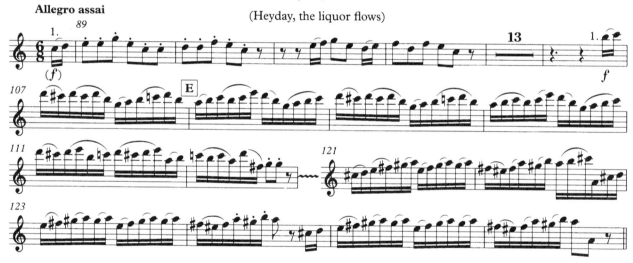

SYMPHONY NO. 62 IN D MAJOR

2nd Movement

HAYDN

SYMPHONY NO. 72 IN D MAJOR

2nd Movement

HAYDN

4th Movement: Finale

86

SYMPHONY NO. 73 IN D MAJOR

'La Chasse'

4th Movement

Take care with the high D which is often flat: perhaps try alternate fingerings.

HAYDN

SYMPHONY NO. 76 IN E♭ MAJOR

2nd Movement

HAYDN

SYMPHONY NO. 81 IN G MAJOR

2nd Movement

HAYDN

SYMPHONY NO. 82 IN C MAJOR

'L'Ours' ('The Bear')

2nd Movement

HAYDN

SYMPHONY NO. 85 IN B♭ MAJOR

'La reine'

2nd Movement: Romance

HAYDN

SYMPHONY NO. 86 IN D MAJOR

2nd Movement

HAYDN

Allegro con spirito

4th Movement: Finale

(with oboe to bar 97)

HAYDN

89

SYMPHONY NO. 92 IN G MAJOR

'The Oxford'

1st Movement

HAYDN

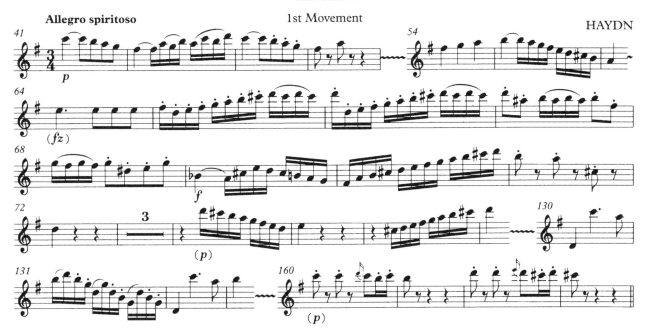

SYMPHONY NO. 94 IN G MAJOR

'The Surprise'

1st Movement

HAYDN

4th Movement: Finale

HAYDN

SYMPHONY NO. 101 IN D MAJOR

'The Clock'

1st Movement

HAYDN

90

2nd Movement

3rd Movement

4th Movement

SYMPHONY NO. 102 IN B♭ MAJOR

1st Movement

HAYDN

2nd Movement

SYMPHONY NO. 103 IN E♭ MAJOR

'The Drum Roll'

1st Movement

HAYDN

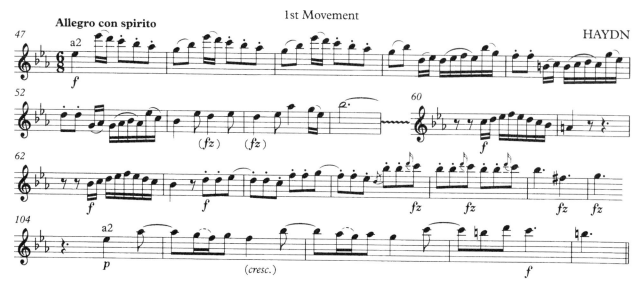

2nd Movement

SYMPHONY NO. 104 IN D MAJOR

'The London'

1st Movement

HAYDN

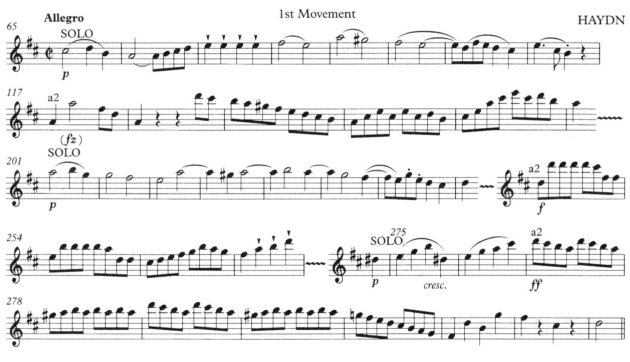

2nd Movement

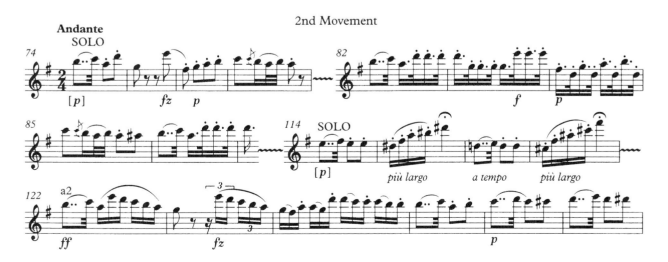

4th Movement: Finale

Any booking you may get for a concert which includes a Mozart Piano Concerto should send you scurrying hotfoot for a score. The clarity of the writing is such that you will need to play with neatness and beautiful phrasing, particularly the ornaments, trills, etc. Here are some important examples. The tunes in the *allegros* are often shared with the first violins and other solos shared with the solo wind.

The South German, or Viennese grand piano, for which Mozart wrote his works, has a lighter and more silvery tone than today's Steinway or Bösendorfer. Performances on modern pianos are mirrored in our heavier and louder style of flute playing, but take care! There is an increasing demand for historically inspired performances which themselves demand the appropriate solo instrument on which to perform the concerto. In the future, perhaps the orchestral player will be required to reflect the use of a softer and more pertinent instrument for Mozart.

PIANO CONCERTO IN G MAJOR, K.453

2nd Movement

MOZART

PIANO CONCERTO IN E♭ MAJOR, K.482

2nd Movement

MOZART

PIANO CONCERTO IN C MINOR, K.491

2nd Movement

MOZART

PIANO CONCERTO IN C MAJOR, K.503

2nd Movement

MOZART

PIANO CONCERTO IN D MAJOR, K.537

'Coronation'

3rd Movement

MOZART

MASS IN C MINOR, K.427

Credo. Et incarnatus est

MOZART

98

COSÌ FAN TUTTE, K.588

Overture

MOZART

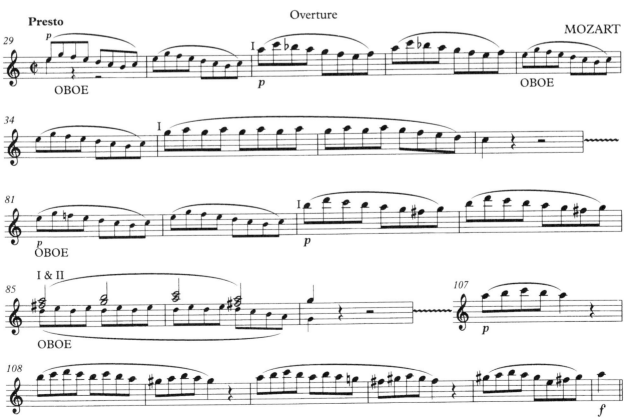

DIE ZAUBERFLÖTE

Overture

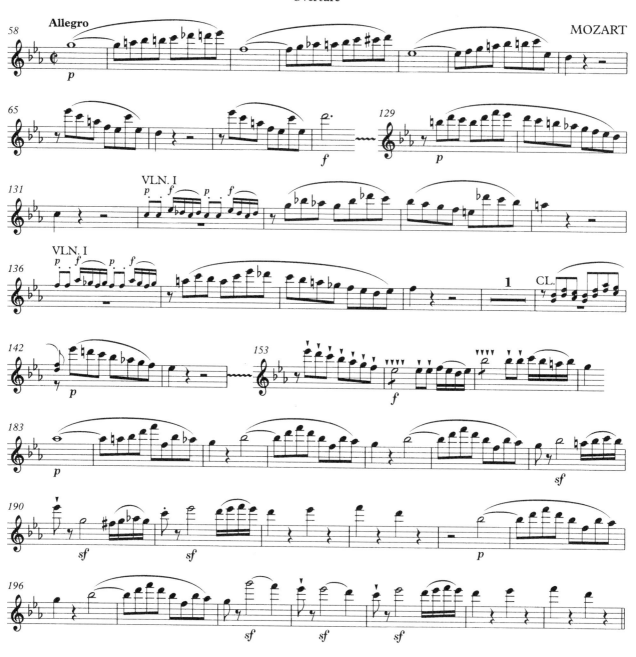

SERENADE NO. 9 IN D, K.320

'Posthorn'

Menuetto: Trio

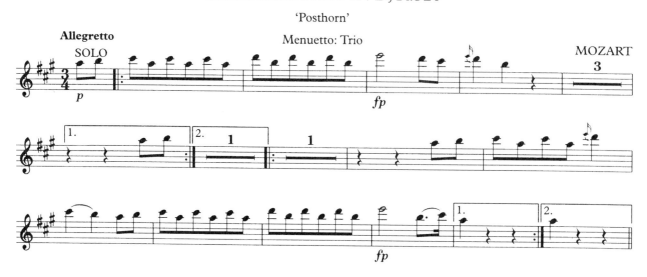

Concertante

Rondo

SYMPHONY NO. 31 IN D MAJOR, K.297

'Paris'

2nd Movement

MOZART

SYMPHONY NO. 38 IN D MAJOR, K.504

'Prague'

2nd Movement

MOZART

SYMPHONY NO. 39 IN E♭, K.543

1st Movement

MOZART

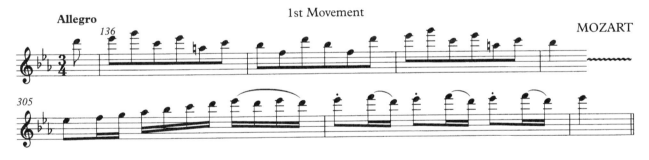

4th Movement

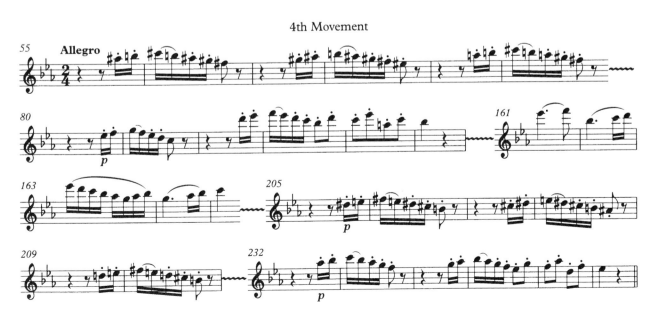

SYMPHONY NO. 40 IN G MINOR, K.550

1st Movement

MOZART

2nd Movement

4th Movement

SYMPHONY NO. 41 IN C MAJOR, K.551

'Jupiter'

1st Movement

MOZART

General Section

We have added some helpful notes where appropriate. We leave the rest to you!

CHRISTMAS ORATORIO

Part 2 15. Aria: Frohe Hirten

Where there are extended passages of demisemiquavers the use of slurs will soften the phrasing. Ornaments must be on the beat, not before.

19. Aria: Schlafe, mein Liebster

(♪ = c.92)

FLUTE

ALTO

wa - che nach die-sem vor al - ler __ Ge - dei-hen, schla - fe, __ mein Lieb-ster, ge - nie - ße der

ST. JOHN PASSION

13. Ich folge dir gleichfalls

BACH

Ich fol - ge _ dir _ gleich-falls mit freu-di - gen Schrit-ten,

Ich

50. Chorus: Schreibe nicht: der Jüden König

This passage is famous for the unexpected. Practise it until you can sail through it without a mistake.

63. Aria: Zerfließe, mein Herze

Zer - flie - ße,___ mein Her-ze, in Flu - ten_ der_ Zäh-ren,

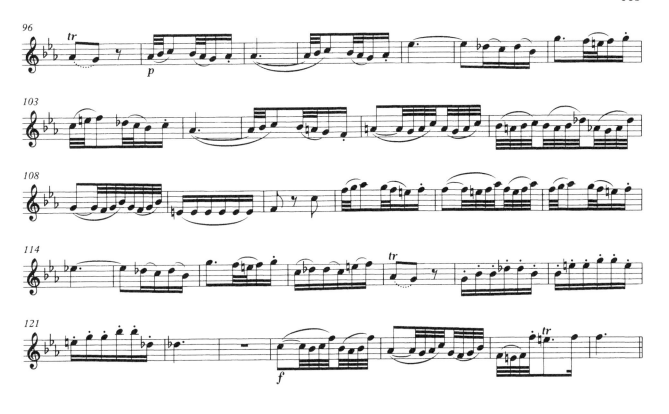

PIANO CONCERTO

1st Movement

BARBER

2nd Movement: Canzone

114

VIOLIN CONCERTO

3rd Movement

BARBER

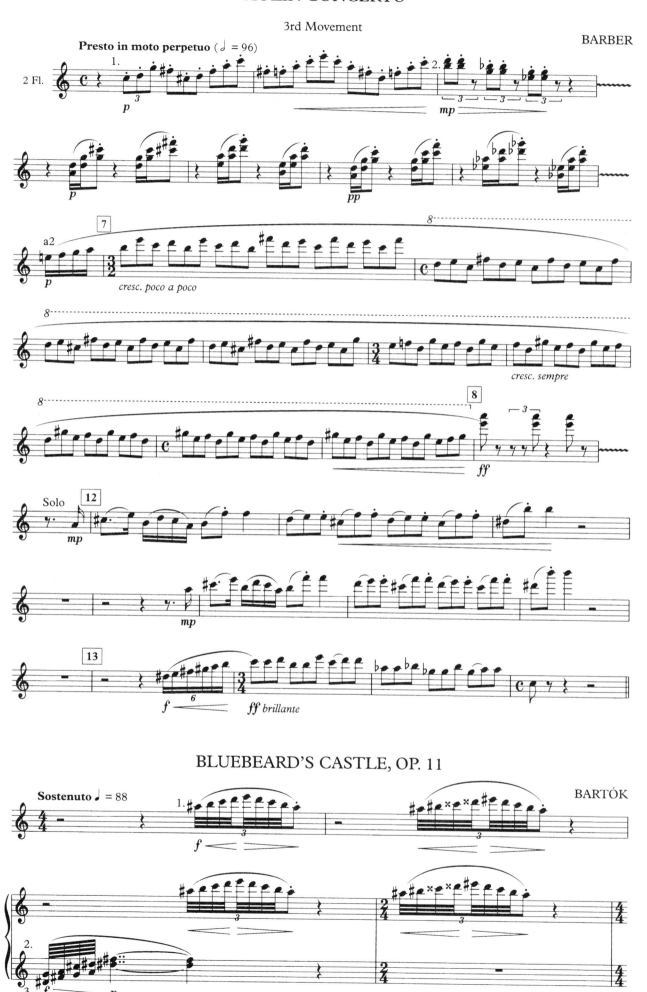

BLUEBEARD'S CASTLE, OP. 11

BARTÓK

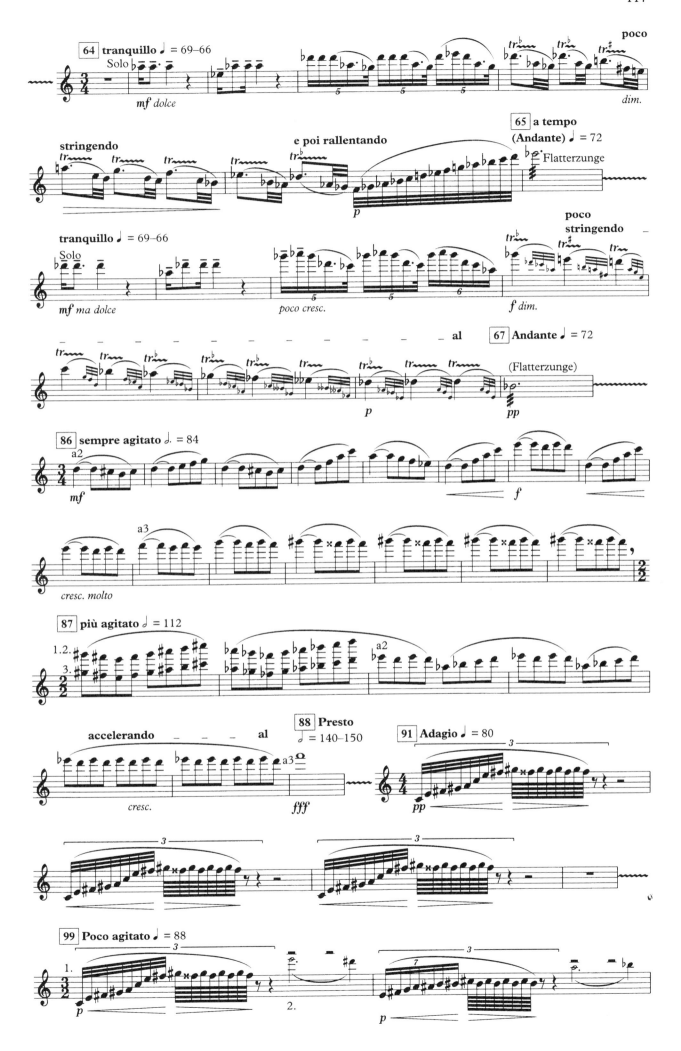

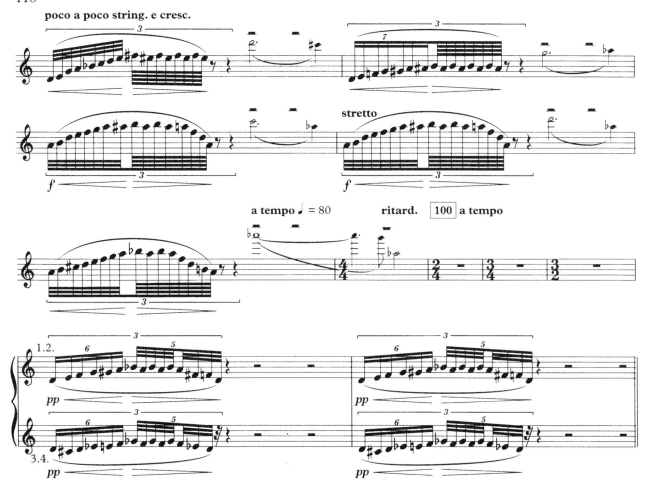

THE MIRACULOUS MANDARIN, OP. 19

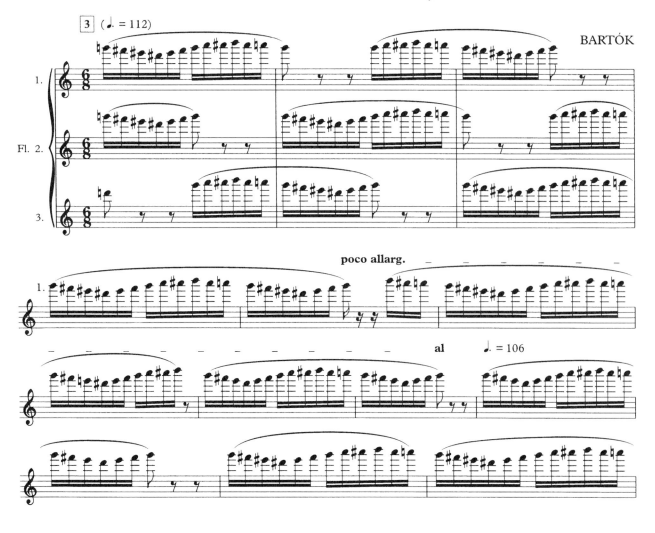

120

PIANO CONCERTO NO. 1

1st Movement

BARTÓK

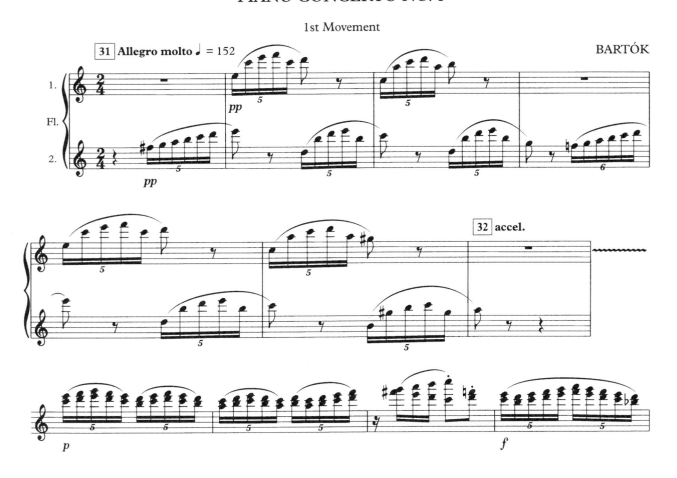

122

PIANO CONCERTO NO. 2

1st Movement

BARTÓK

VIOLIN CONCERTO NO. 2

1st Movement

BARTÓK

THE GARDEN OF FAND

BAX

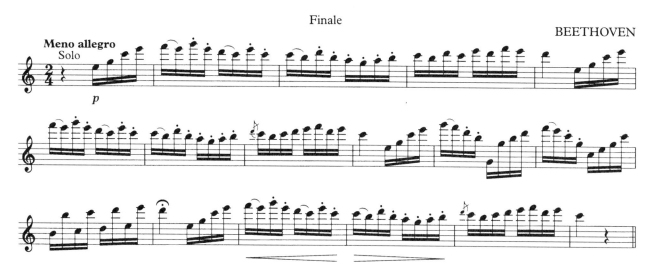
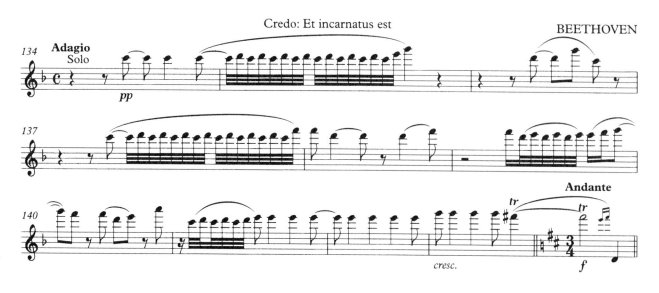

Andante con moto *Gently rhythmical*

CHORAL FANTASY, OP. 80

Finale

BEETHOVEN

Meno allegro
Solo

MISSA SOLEMNIS

Credo: Et incarnatus est

BEETHOVEN

Adagio
Solo

Andante

OVERTURE 'LEONORE NO. 2' *

BEETHOVEN

* See also Section 2, p.29 for No. 3.

ROMANCE IN F, OP. 50

for violin and orchestra

BEETHOVEN

DIE RUINEN VON ATHEN, OP. 113

(THE RUINS OF ATHENS)

Chorus: Tochter des mächtigen Zeus

BEETHOVEN

SYMPHONY NO. 1 IN C MAJOR

2nd Movement

BEETHOVEN

4th Movement

SYMPHONY NO. 3 IN E♭ MAJOR

'Eroica'

2nd Movement: Marcia funebre

BEETHOVEN

3rd Movement: Scherzo

SYMPHONY NO. 4 IN B♭ MAJOR

1st Movement

BEETHOVEN

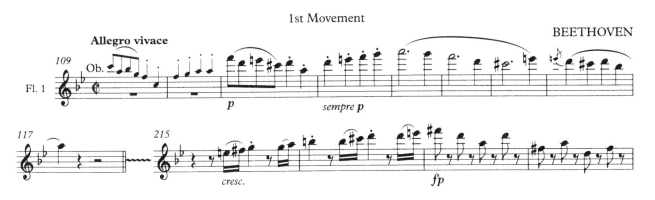

2nd Movement

3rd Movement: Menuetto

SYMPHONY NO. 7 IN A MAJOR

1st Movement

BEETHOVEN

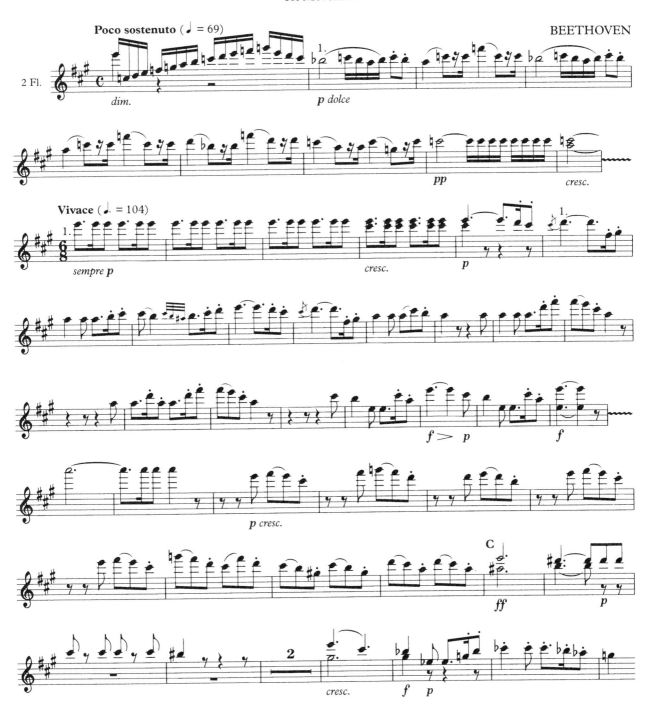

2nd Movement

3rd Movement

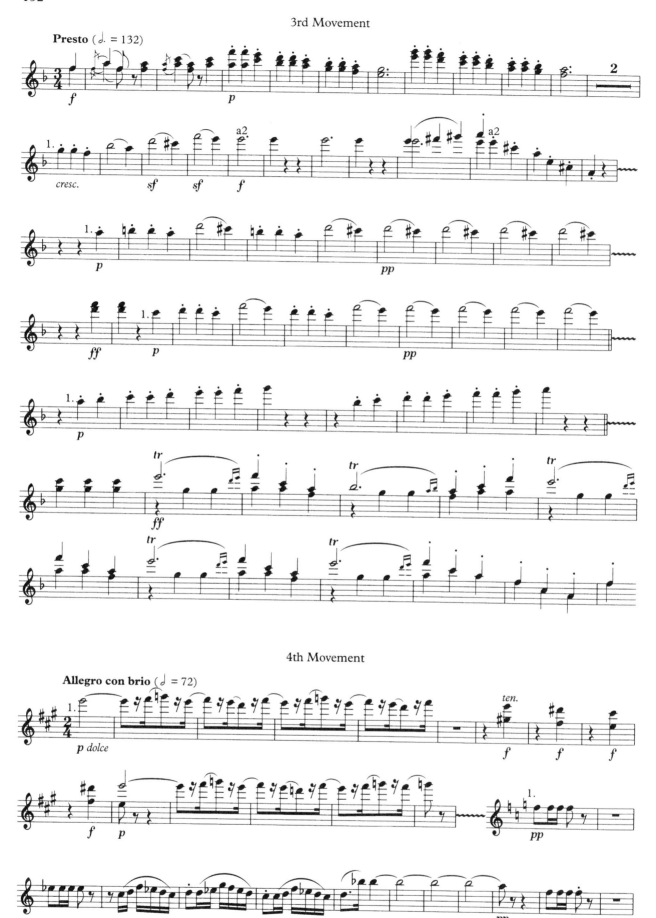

4th Movement

SYMPHONY NO. 8 IN F MAJOR

1st Movement

BEETHOVEN

* Although written at the lower 8ve, these notes are often played an octave up.

SYMPHONY NO. 9 IN D MINOR

1st Movement

BEETHOVEN

2nd Movement

3rd Movement

4th Movement

* Although written at the lower octave, these notes are often played an octave up.

LE CARNAVAL ROMAIN

Overture

BERLIOZ

LA DAMNATION DE FAUST

3ème Partie: Scène XI: Menuet des Follets

Presto e leggiero (♩ = 144)
[with 2 piccolos]

BERLIOZ

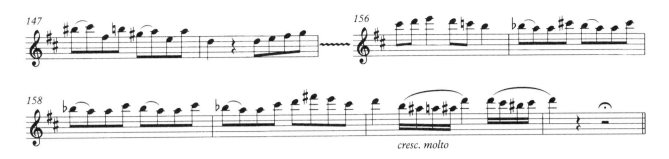

ROMÉO ET JULIETTE

3. Scène d'amour

BERLIOZ

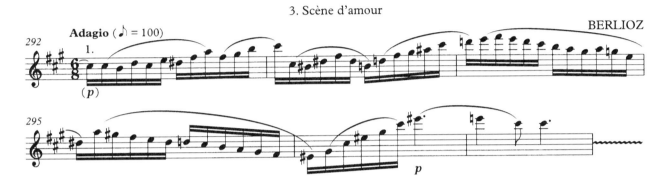

4. La Reine Mab, ou la Fée des Songes

Scherzo

138

5. Convoi funèbre de Juliette

SYMPHONIE FANTASTIQUE

I. Rêveries – Passions

The principal flute may suggest that the second player plays one of the groups of semiquavers (sixteenth-notes) so they can take a breath. The usual two groups are marked with a *.

SYMPHONIC DANCES FROM 'WEST SIDE STORY'

Remember to play in a jazz style. It isn't practical, or necessary, for composers to write jazz rhythms accurately, so players must interpret this style as best they can.

BERNSTEIN

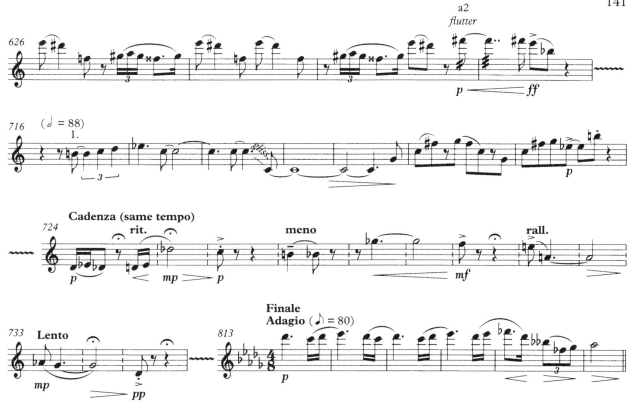

JEUX D'ENFANTS

V. Galop

BIZET

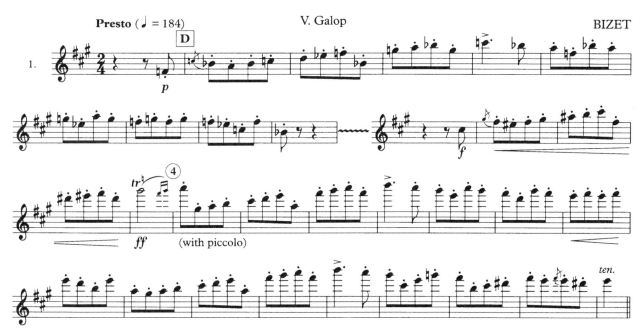

ORCHESTRAL VARIATIONS

on a theme by Paganini

6.

BLACHER

142

POLOVTSIAN DANCES

from 'Prince Igor'

BORODIN

* When this passage is very fast it will be helpful to use trill fingerings here.

144

PIANO CONCERTO NO. 2 IN B♭ MAJOR

1st Movement

BRAHMS

4th Movement

* Open the G♯ key to sharpen the B.

SERENADE NO. 1 IN D MAJOR

2nd Movement

Scherzo

BRAHMS

3rd Movement

6th Movement

Rondo

SERENADE NO. 2 IN A MAJOR

(Revised version, 1875)

1st Movement

BRAHMS

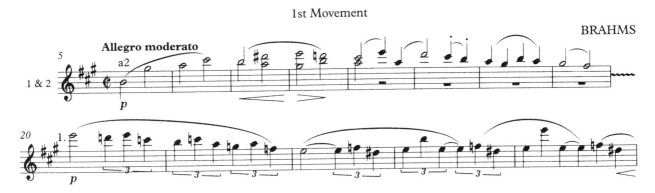

3rd Movement

SYMPHONY NO. 1 IN C MINOR

1st Movement

BRAHMS

2nd Movement

3rd Movement

4th Movement

SYMPHONY NO. 2 IN D MAJOR

1st Movement

BRAHMS

148

2nd Movement

3rd Movement

4th Movement

SYMPHONY NO. 3 IN F MAJOR

1st Movement

BRAHMS

2nd Movement

3rd Movement

4th Movement

VARIATIONS ON A THEME BY HAYDN

Var. III

BRAHMS

Var. IV

Var. VIII

VIOLIN CONCERTO IN D MAJOR

1st Movement

BRAHMS

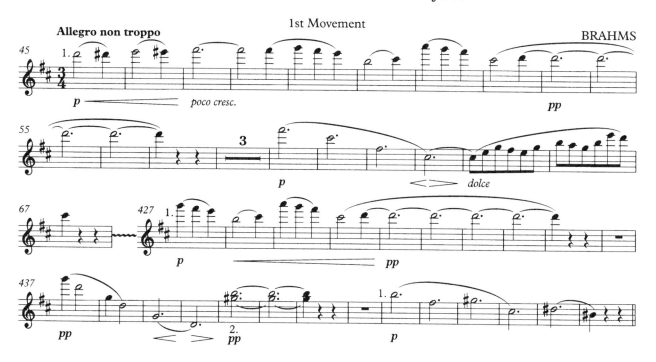

FOUR SEA-INTERLUDES

from the Opera 'Peter Grimes'

In No. 1 the flutes are in unison with the violins. Pitching the Es is the problem.

I Dawn

II Sunday Morning

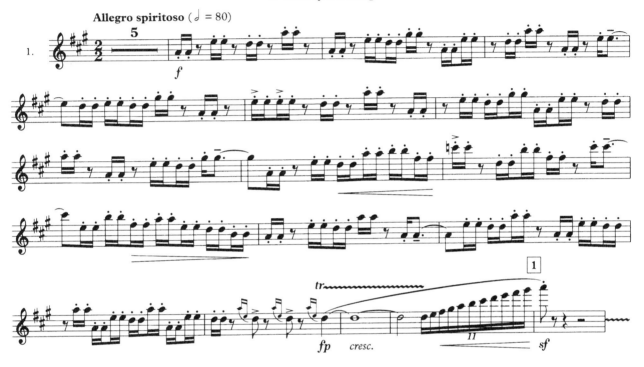

III Moonlight

IV Storm

SINFONIETTA, OP. 1

1st Movement

BRITTEN

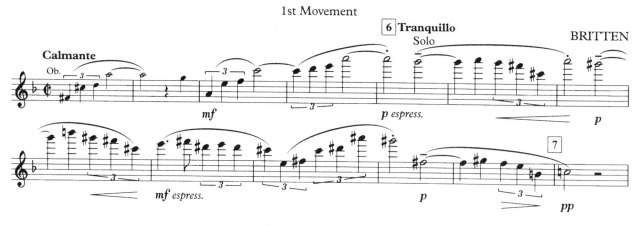

2nd Movement: Variations

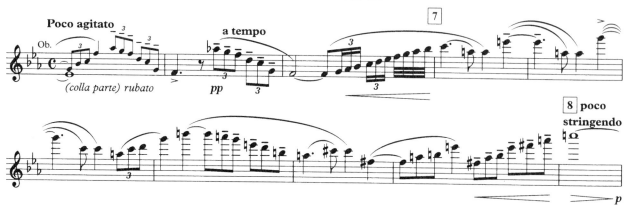

3rd Movement: Tarantella

SCOTTISH FANTASIE, OP. 46

for violin and orchestra

2nd Movement

This is with the solo violin: it needs to be flexible – the amount of flexibility will depend on the violinist.

[Allegro ♩ = 116]
1. Solo

BRUCH

APPALACHIAN SPRING

Suite

COPLAND

BILLY THE KID

Ballet-Suite

Introduction: The Open Prairie

COPLAND

Scene 1a: Street in a Frontier Town

HOE-DOWN

from 'Rodeo'

COPLAND

LA DAMOISELLE ÉLUE

DEBUSSY

IBERIA

I. Par les rues et par les chemins

DEBUSSY

II. Les parfums de la nuit

III. Le matin d'un jour de fête

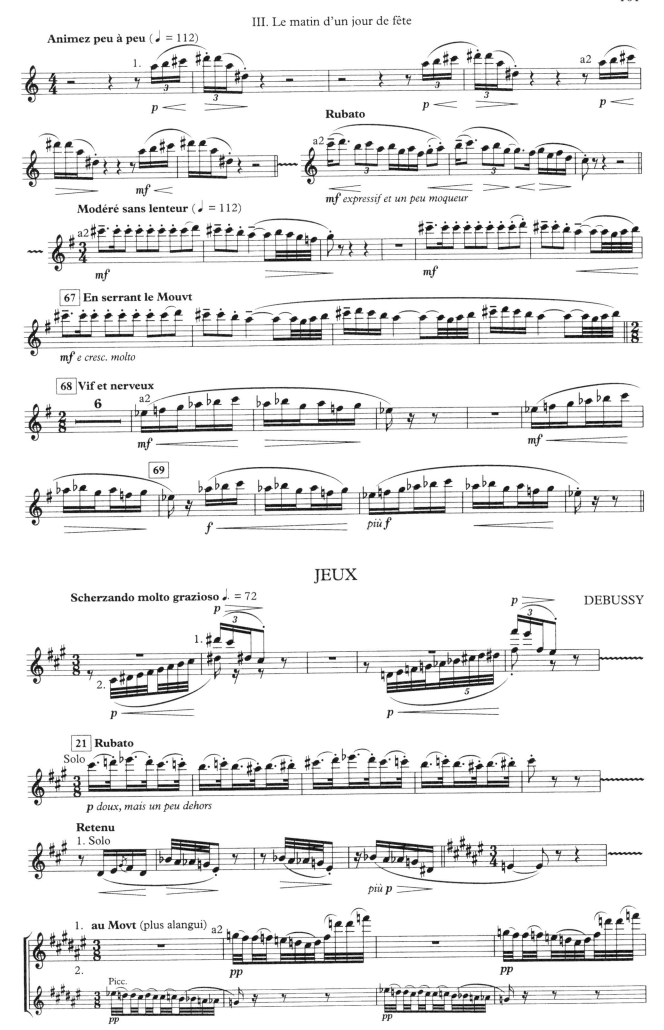

JEUX

DEBUSSY

LA MER

I. De l'aube à midi sur la mer

DEBUSSY

II. Jeux de vagues

III. Dialogue du vent et de la mer

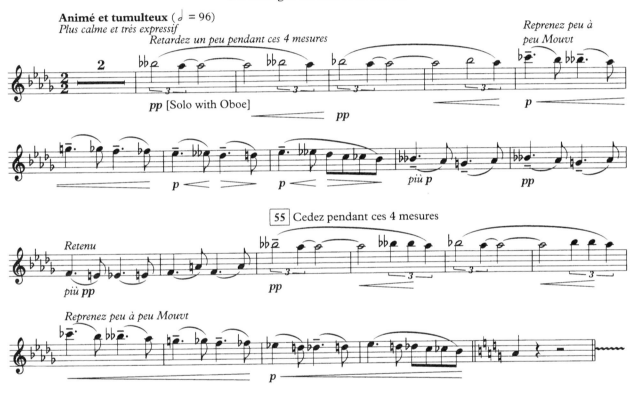

NOCTURNES

1. Nuages

DEBUSSY

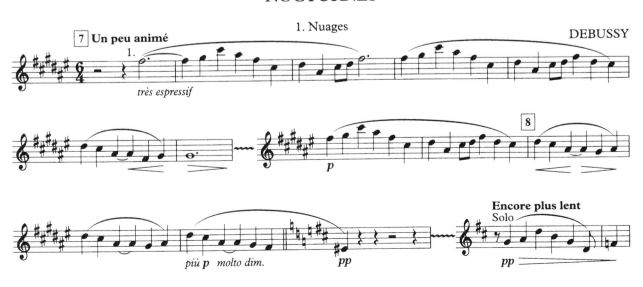

2. Fêtes

RONDES DE PRINTEMPS

DEBUSSY

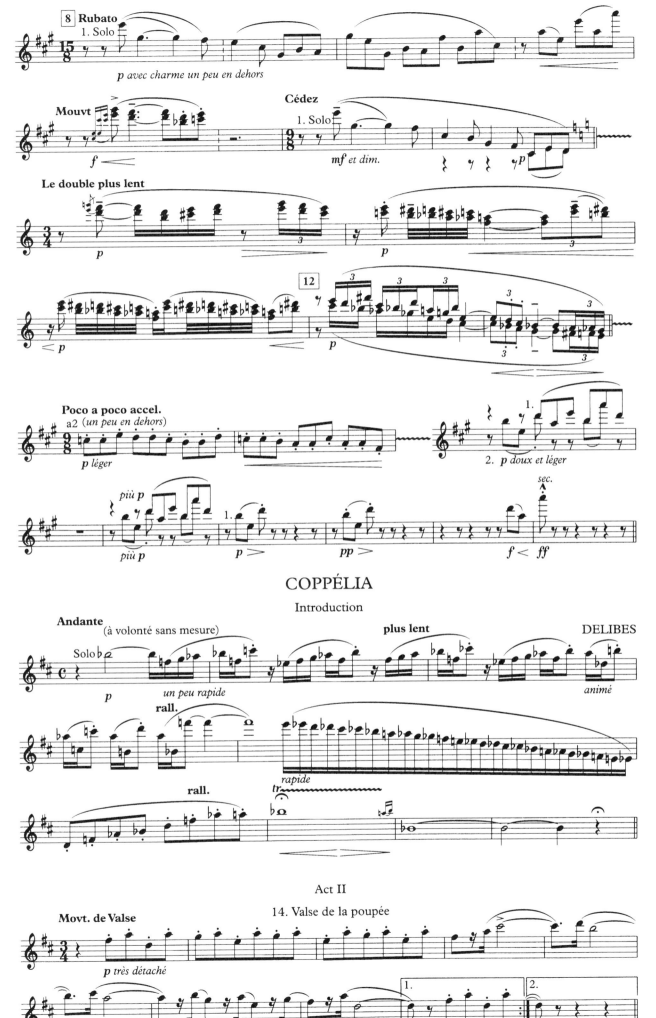

COPPÉLIA

Introduction

DELIBES

Act II

14. Valse de la poupée

17. Gigue

VARIATIONS ON A NURSERY SONG, OP. 25

for piano and orchestra

Var. IV

The solo is in octaves with the piccolo – watch the tuning!

DOHNÁNYI

L'APPRENTI SORCIER

(The Sorcerer's Apprentice)

The first time this was encountered, the section principal was asked how much of it he played accurately. He replied, 'I'm not sure I played *all* the notes, but I played the *effect* of all the notes!' The fast section can go very fast indeed!

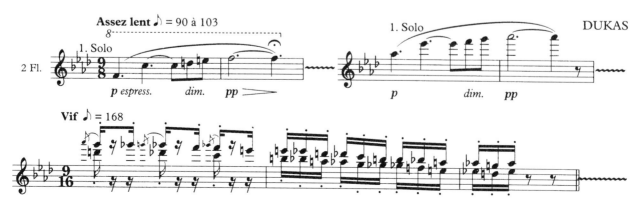

DUKAS

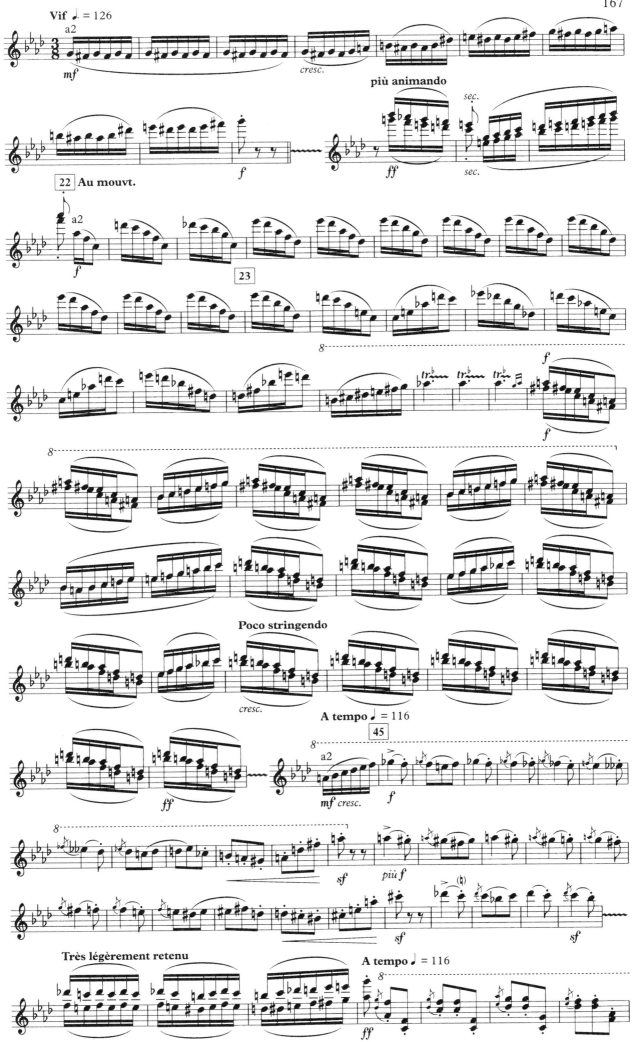

CELLO CONCERTO IN B MINOR, OP. 104

DVOŘÁK

2nd Movement

3rd Movement: Finale

KARNEVAL

Concert Overture, Op. 92

DVOŘÁK

SLAVONIC DANCES, OP. 46

Here is a selection of passages from these dances: they are all a little tricky so be warned!

I

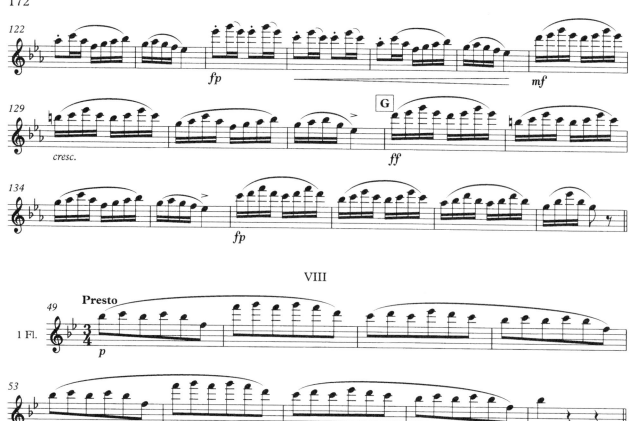

VIII

SLAVONIC DANCES, OP. 72

2

DVOŘÁK

SYMPHONY NO. 5 IN F MAJOR, OP. 76 *

1st Movement

Allegro, ma non troppo ♩ = 112

DVOŘÁK

2nd Movement

* This work was first published as Symphony No. 3

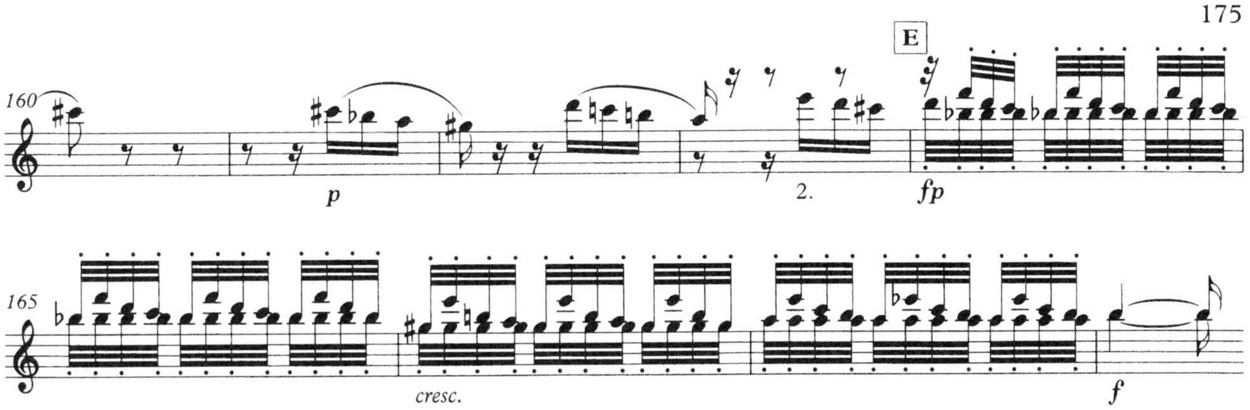

3rd Movement

SYMPHONY NO. 7 IN D MINOR, OP. 70*

1st Movement

DVOŘÁK

* This work was first published as Symphony No. 2

176

2nd Movement

3rd Movement: Scherzo

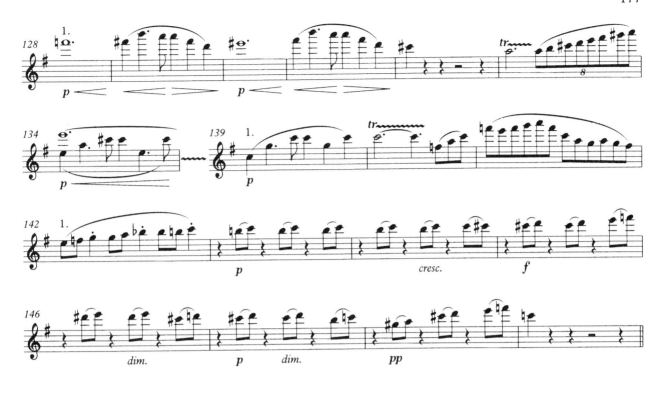

4th Movement

NURSERY SUITE

2. The Serious Doll

ELGAR

179

THE WAND OF YOUTH, SUITE NO. 2

II. The Little Bells

(Scherzino)

ELGAR

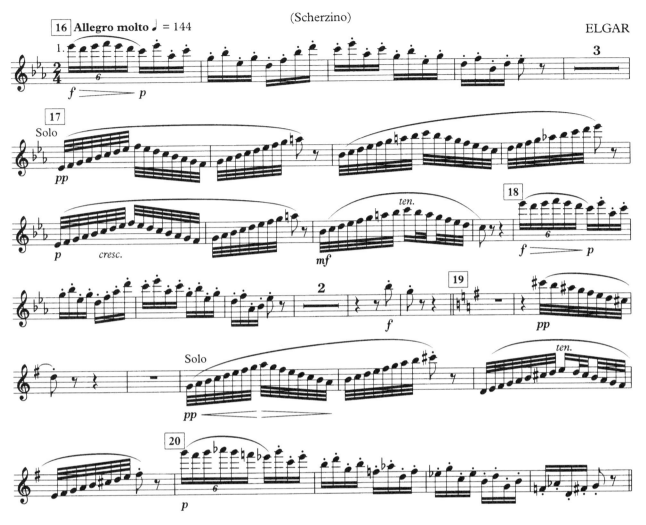

NOCHES EN LOS JARDINES DE ESPAÑA

for piano and orchestra

II. Danza lejana

FALLA

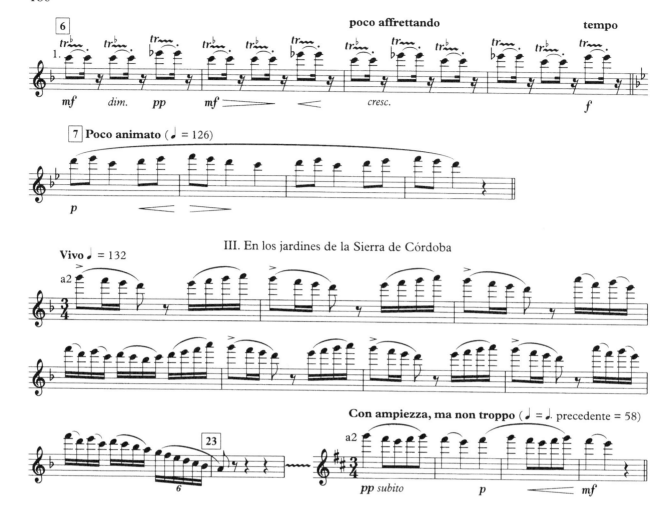

III. En los jardines de la Sierra de Córdoba

PELLÉAS ET MÉLISANDE SUITE

III. Sicilienne

FAURÉ

THE SEASONS, OP. 67

1ᵉʳ Tableau

GLAZUNOV

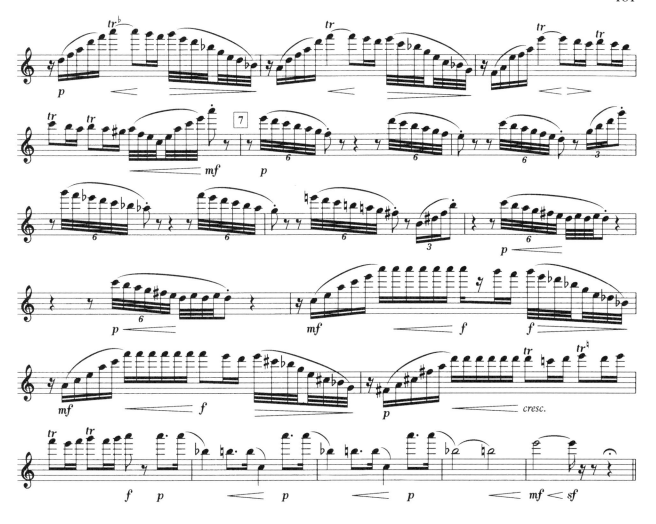

VIOLIN CONCERTO IN A MINOR, OP. 82

GLAZUNOV

182

HARMONIE DER WELT

I. Musica Instrumentalis

HINDEMITH

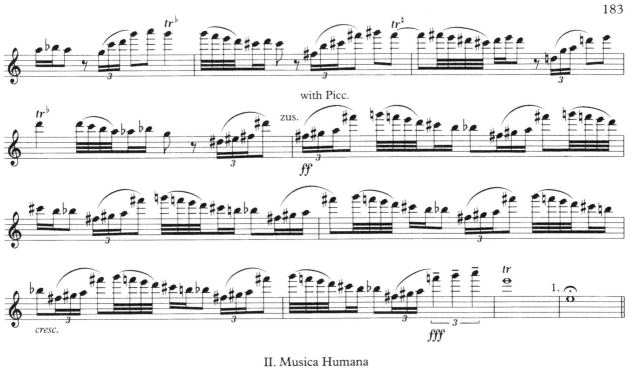

II. Musica Humana

184

III. Musica mundana

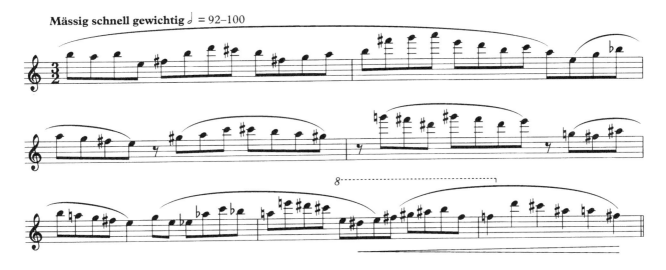

THE PLANETS

I. Mars, the Bringer of War

HOLST

186

III. Mercury, the Winged Messenger

IV. Jupiter, the Bringer of Jollity

VI. Uranus, the Magician

VII. Neptune the Mystic

Not too much vibrato; this is with the 2nd flute and alto.

DIVERTISSEMENT

for chamber orchestra

I. Introduction

IBERT

188

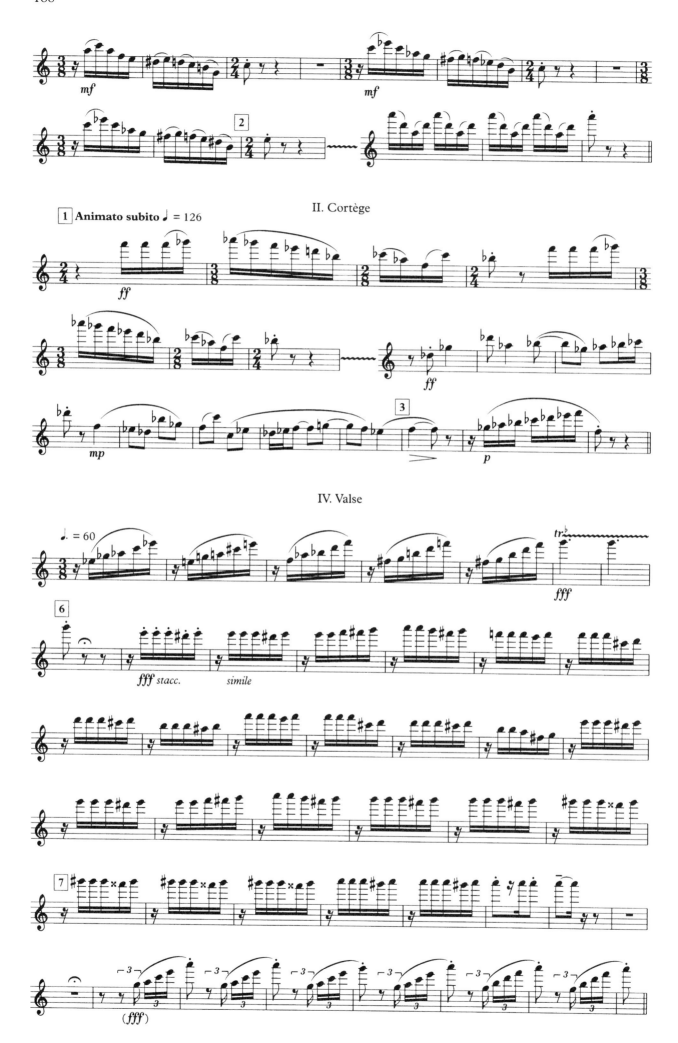

II. Cortège

1 Animato subito ♩ = 126

IV. Valse

ESQUISSES CAUCASIENNES, OP. 10

4. Cortège du Sardar

IPPOLITOV-IVANOV

SINFONIETTA

3rd Movement

JANÁČEK

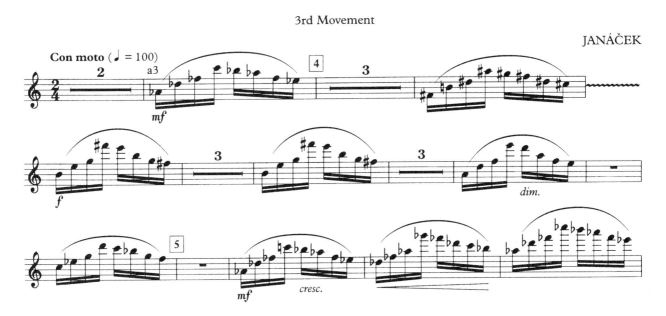

190

COLAS BREUGNON

Overture

This isn't a popular piece, though you may well come across it in an orchestral career. It is included for the excellent top note practice it provides, and it will be fruitful to work at it as an exercise, in conjunction with Prokofiev's Classical Symphony. For fast scales up to and including top C, try the standard B fingering but take off your thumb: this note is nearer to the true pitch of C than the usual fingering.

KABALEVSKY

HÁRY JÁNOS SUITE

II. Viennese Musical Clock

KODÁLY

III. Song

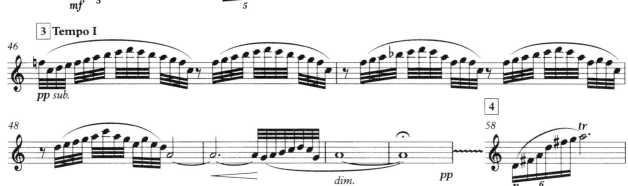

V. Intermezzo

VI. Entrance of the Emperor and his Court

DANCES OF MAROSSZÉK

KODÁLY

* This continues for a further 11 bars of 'F', with a *diminuendo* to the end.
** The difficulty here is that the flute's 6/8 bars have to fit over 4/8 in the strings – and these bars are conducted in 4/8! It may help to set your metronome to 4 beats and focus your mind on every beat – and play your 6/8 bars to this.

DANCES OF GALÁNTA

KODÁLY

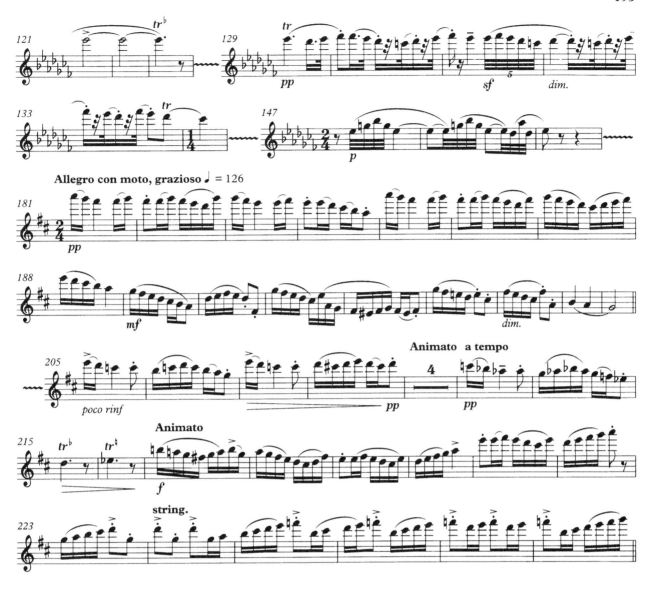

PIANO CONCERTO NO. 1

2nd Movement

LISZT

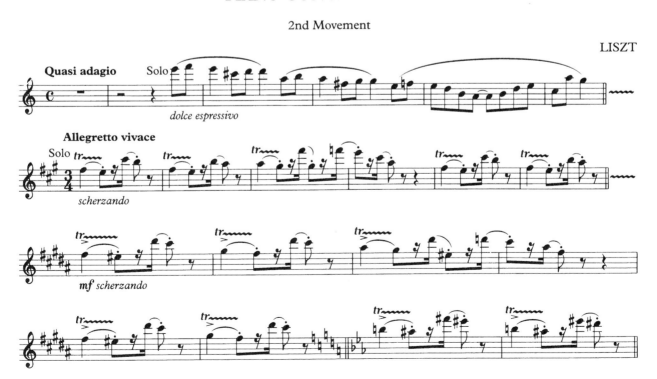

8 CHANTS POPULAIRES RUSSES, OP. 58

IV. Chant comique: J'ai dansé avec le moucheron

LYADOV

OVERTURE 'RUY BLAS'

MENDELSSOHN

VIOLIN CONCERTO IN E MINOR

3rd Movement

MENDELSSOHN

SYMPHONY NO. 3 IN A MINOR

'The Scottish'

1st Movement

MENDELSSOHN

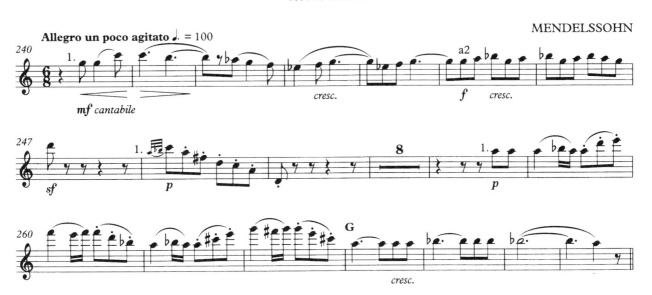

2nd Movement

4th Movement

OVERTURE 'CALM SEA AND PROSPEROUS VOYAGE'

MENDELSSOHN

200

A MIDSUMMER NIGHT'S DREAM

Act IV. Nocturne

MENDELSSOHN

LE BŒUF SUR LE TOIT

MILHAUD

201

PICTURES FROM AN EXHIBITION

III. Tuileries

MUSORGSKY
Orch. Ravel

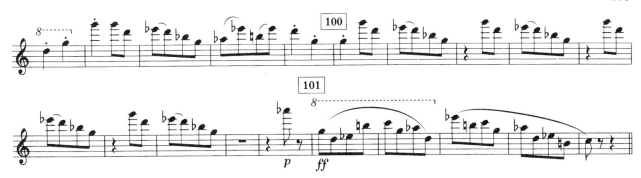

KHOVANSHCHINA

Introduction

MUSORGSKY
Orch. Rimsky-Korsakov

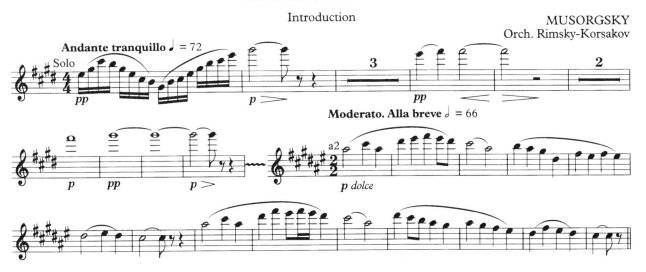

THE MERRY WIVES OF WINDSOR

Overture

NICOLAI

THE INCREDIBLE FLUTIST

Ballet Suite

Entrance of the Vendors

PISTON

The Flutist

Polka Finale

LA GIOCONDA

Act III: Dance of the Hours

PONCHIELLI

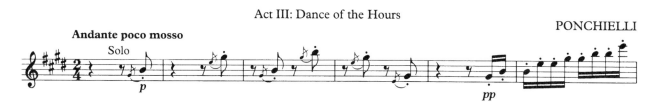

VIOLIN CONCERTO NO. 1 IN D MAJOR

1st Movement

PROKOFIEV

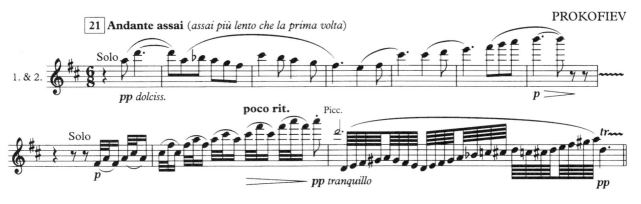

2nd Movement: Scherzo

LIEUTENANT KIJÉ

2. Romance

PROKOFIEV

5. Interment of Kijé

CLASSICAL SYMPHONY

PROKOFIEV

In the last movement, (Figure 50) there are a number of ways of making life easier in the passages with two flutes, with the agreement of your colleague. Here are two:

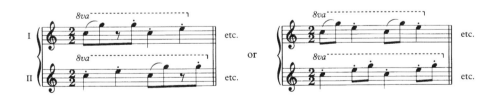

Whichever you choose, you will need to write the two passages out fully in both keys, and then practise them; the trick of it is to ensure the notes are uniformly short and exactly together. It would be very difficult for anyone to detect the difference. All the same, you will need to learn the passage using the correct notation for an audition!

1st Movement

2nd Movement

3rd Movement: Gavotta

4th Movement: Finale

209

* ** For alternative fingering for this passage, see page 210.

210

Alternative fingerings:

Or try:

or try:

PIANO CONCERTO NO. 3 IN C MAJOR

1st Movement

PROKOFIEV

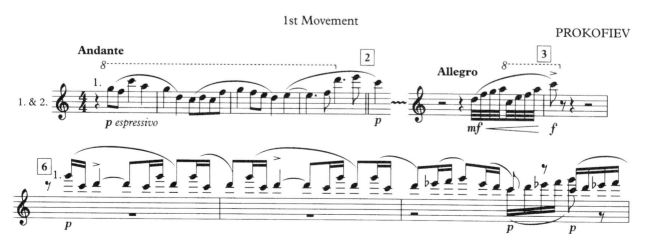

2nd Movement

INDEX

ACKNOWLEDGEMENTS

Extracts from the following works are reprinted by permission of the publishers concerned. (We have endeavoured to trace all copyright holders but will be pleased to rectify any omissions notified to us in future reprints.)

Barber Piano Concerto	Copyright © 1962 (Renewed) by G. Schirmer, Inc. (ASCAP). International Copyright Secured. All Rights Reserved.
Barber Violin Concerto	Copyright © 1956 (Renewed) by G. Schirmer, Inc. (ASCAP). International Copyright Secured. All Rights Reserved.
Bartók Bluebeard's Castle, Op.11	© Copyright 1925 by Universal Edition A.G., Wien. Copyright renewed 1952 by Boosey & Hawkes, Inc.
Bartók Concerto for Orchestra	© Copyright 1946 by Hawkes & Son (London) Ltd. Reproduced by permission of Boosey & Hawkes Music Publishers Ltd.
Bartók The Miraculous Mandarin	Copyright 1927 by Universal Edition. Copyright renewed 1955 by Boosey & Hawkes, Inc., New York.
Bartók Piano Concerto No.1	Copyright 1927 by Universal Edition. Copyright renewed 1954 by Boosey & Hawkes, Inc., New York.
Bartók Piano Concerto No.2	© Copyright 1932 by Universal Edition A.G., Wien. All rights in the USA owned and controlled by Boosey & Hawkes, Inc., New York.
Bartók Violin Concerto No.2	© Copyright 1946 by Hawkes & Son (London) Ltd. Reproduced by permission of Boosey & Hawkes Music Publishers Ltd.
Bax The Garden of Fand	© 1927 Murdoch Murdoch & Co, UK. Chappell Music Ltd, London W1Y 3FA. Used by permission of International Music Publications Limited.
Bernstein Symphonic Dances from 'West Side Story'	© Copyright 1967 by the Estate of Leonard Bernstein. Revised edition © 1995 by the Estate of Leonard Bernstein.
Blacher Orchestral Variations	© 1947, renewed 1975 Bote & Bock, Berlin. Used by permission.
Britten Four Sea Interludes	© Copyright 1945 by Boosey & Hawkes Music Publishers Ltd. Reproduced by permission of Boosey & Hawkes Music Publishers Ltd.
Britten Nocturne	© Copyright 1959 by Hawkes & Son (London) Ltd. Reproduced by permission of Boosey & Hawkes Music Publishers Ltd.
Britten Sinfonietta Op.1	© Copyright 1935 by Hawkes & Son (London) Ltd. Reproduced by permission of Boosey & Hawkes Music Publishers Ltd.
Copland Appalachian Spring	© Copyright 1958 the Aaron Copland Fund For Music, Inc. Boosey & Hawkes, Sole Licensee. Reproduced by permission of Boosey & Hawkes Music Publishers Ltd.
Copland Billy the Kid	© Copyright 1978 The Aaron Copland Fund For Music, Inc. Boosey & Hawkes, Sole Licensee. Reproduced by permission of Boosey & Hawkes Music Publishers Ltd.
Copland Hoe-Down from Rodeo	© Copyright 1941 by Aaron Copland. Sole agents for all countries of the World: Boosey & Hawkes Inc. Reproduced by permission of Boosey & Hawkes Music Publishers Ltd.
Delius Dance Rhapsody No.2	© 1923 Stainer & Bell Ltd. Reprinted by kind permission.
Delius Song of Summer	© Copyright 1931 by Hawkes & Son (London) Ltd. Reproduced by permission of Boosey & Hawkes Music Publishers Ltd.
Dohnányi Variations on a Nursery Song	Reprinted by permission of N. Simrock/Richard Schauer Music Publishers London-Hamburg.
Dukas L'Apprenti Sorcier	Reproduced by permission of Editions Durand SA, Paris/ United Music Publishers Ltd.
Elgar Enigma Variations	© Copyright 1899 Novello & Company Limited.
Elgar Nursery Suite: The Serious Doll	© 1931, Reproduced by permission of Keith Prowse Music Pub Co Ltd, London WC2H 0EA.
Elgar The Wand of Youth, Suite No.2	© Copyright 1908 Novello & Company Limited.
Falla Nights in the Gardens of Spain	Reproduced by permission of Editions Max Eschig, Paris/United Music Publishers Ltd.
Fauré Pavane	Reproduced by permission of Editions Hamelle, Paris/United Music Publishers Ltd.
Fauré Sicilienne from Pelléas et Mélisande Suite	Reproduced by permission of Editions Hamelle, Paris/United Music Publishers Ltd.
Glazunov The Seasons Op.67	© 1973 by MP Belaieff, Frankfurt. Reproduced on behalf of the Publishers by permission of Peters Edition Limited, London.
Glazunov Violin Concerto in A Minor	© 1936 by MP Belaieff, Frankfurt. © renewed 1964 by MP Belaieff. Reproduced on behalf of the Publishers by permission of Peters Edition Ltd, London.
Hindemith Harmonie der Welt	© Schott & Co. Ltd., London, 1952. © renewed 1980.
Hindemith Symphonic Metamorphoses	© by Associated Music Publishers Inc., New York, 1945. © assigned 1964 to B. Schott's Söhne, Mainz. © renewed 1973.
Holst The Planets	© Copyright 1921 Goodwin and Tabb; transferred to J. Curwen & Sons Limited.
Ibert Divertissement	Reproduced by permission of Editions Durand S.A, Paris/United Music Publishers Ltd. Sole representative USA & Canada Theodore Presser Company.
Janácek Sinfonietta	Copyright 1927 by Universal Edition. Copyright renewed 1954.
Kabalevsky Colas Breugnon	© Copyright 1941 by Boosey & Hawkes Music Publishers Ltd. Reproduced by permission of Boosey & Hawkes Music Publishers Ltd.
Kodály Dances of Galánta	Copyright 1934 by Universal Edition A.G. Copyright assigned 1952 to Universal Edition (London) Ltd., London. Copyright renewed 1962.